SPSS® 6.1 for Windows™ Brief Guide

SPSS Inc.

SPSS Inc.
444 N. Michigan Avenue
Chicago, Illinois 60611
Tel: (312) 329-2400
Fax: (312) 329-3668

SPSS Federal Systems (U.S.)
SPSS Latin America
SPSS Benelux BV
SPSS GmbH Software
SPSS Hellas SA
SPSS UK Ltd.
SPSS France SARL
SPSS Hispanoportuguesa S.L.
SPSS Scandinavia AB
SPSS Italia srl
SPSS Israel Ltd.
SPSS India Private Ltd.
SPSS Asia Pacific Pte. Ltd.
SPSS Japan Inc.
SPSS Australasia Pty. Ltd.

For more information about SPSS® software products, please write or call

Marketing Department
SPSS Inc.
444 North Michigan Avenue
Chicago, IL 60611
Tel: (312) 329-2400
Fax: (312) 329-3668

SPSS® 6.1 for Windows™ Brief Guide

Published by Prentice-Hall, Inc.
A Simon & Schuster Company
Englewood Cliffs, New Jersey 07632

Printed in the United States of America.

1 2 3 4 5 6 7 8 9 0   99 98 97 96 95

ISBN 0-13-455677-1

Library of Congress Catalog Card Number: 95-069474

Preface

SPSS is a comprehensive and flexible statistical analysis and data management system. SPSS can take data from almost any type of file and use them to generate tabulated reports, charts and plots of distributions and trends, descriptive statistics, and complex statistical analyses.

SPSS for Windows provides a user interface that makes statistical analysis more accessible for the casual user and more convenient for the experienced user. Simple menus and dialog box selections make it possible to perform complex analyses without typing a single line of command syntax. The Data Editor offers a simple and efficient spreadsheet-like facility for entering data and browsing the working data file. High-resolution, presentation-quality charts and plots are included as part of the Base system.

The *SPSS 6.1 for Windows Brief Guide* provides a set of tutorials designed to acquaint you with the various components of the SPSS system. You can work through the tutorials in sequence or turn to the topics for which you need additional information. You can use this book as a supplement to the online tutorial that is included with the SPSS 6.1 system or ignore the online tutorial and start in with the tutorials found here.

Sample Data

The data used for all but one example in this book are from a file named *employee.sav;* the time series example uses a file named *inventry.sav.* These files are included with the Student Version of SPSS 6.1 for Windows and are also available from the publisher, Prentice Hall; ask for the SPSS for Windows Data Disk.

The files are also available through the following methods:

SPSS Bulletin Board. You can also download the files from the SPSS Bulletin Board:

Configuration:	8/N/1 9600
Phone:	(312) 836-1900
Name:	Brief Guide
Location:	Files for Customers
Description:	Self-extracting program that opens and saves 2 data *(.sav)* files to your system

Simply double-click on the *Brief.exe* icon from your File Manager.

Anonymous ftp. The files are also available for anonymous ftp at spss.com. The location is */pub/spss/sample/datasets* and the filename is *brief.exe*.

SPSS CompuServe forum. The files are also available in *brief.exe* on the SPSS CompuServe forum.

Alternate File. Finally, if you are using the full (not student) version of SPSS 6.1, a demonstration data file named *bank.sav* was probably installed with your SPSS system. You can use this file in place of *employee.sav,* but you will need to be aware that salaries in the data are different (and so results will be different) and that the following variable names have changed:

Former Name	New Name
employee.sav	*bank.sav*
salary	*salnow*
salbegin	*salbeg*
gender	*sex*
genrace	*sexrace*
race	*minority*
jobtime	*time*
prevexp	*work*

For additional information about the features and operations of SPSS 6.1, you can consult the *SPSS 6.1 for Windows Base System User's Guide*.

Beneath the menus and dialog boxes, SPSS uses a command language, and some extended features of the system can be accessed only via command syntax. (Those features are not available in the Student Version.) Complete command syntax is documented in the *SPSS Base System Syntax Reference Guide*.

SPSS Options

The following options are available as add-on enhancements to the full (not Student Version) SPSS Base system:

SPSS Professional Statistics™ provides techniques to measure the similarities and differences in data, classify data, identify underlying dimensions, and more. It includes procedures for these analyses: cluster, k-means cluster, discriminant, factor, multidimensional scaling, proximity, and reliability.

SPSS Advanced Statistics™ includes sophisticated techniques such as logistic regression, loglinear analysis, multivariate analysis of variance, constrained nonlinear regression, probit analysis, Cox regression, and Kaplan-Meier and actuarial survival analysis.

SPSS Exact Tests™ always calculates reliable *p* values for the test statistics in the Crosstabs and Nonparametric Tests procedures, even when you have a small data set.

SPSS Tables™ creates a variety of presentation-quality tabular reports, including complex tables and displays of multiple response data.

SPSS Trends™ performs comprehensive forecasting and time series analyses with multiple curve-fitting models, smoothing models, and methods for estimating autoregressive functions.

SPSS Categories™ performs conjoint analysis and optimal scaling procedures, including correspondence analysis.

SPSS CHAID™ simplifies tabular analysis of categorical data, develops predictive models, screens out extraneous predictor variables, and produces easy-to-read tree diagrams that segment a population into subgroups that share similar characteristics.

SPSS LISREL® 7 analyzes linear structural relations and simultaneous equation models.

You can expand the system yourself by incorporating programs written in C or FORTRAN. Contact SPSS Inc. for SPSS for Windows User Code documentation.

Training Seminars

SPSS Inc. provides both public and onsite training seminars for SPSS for Windows. All seminars feature hands-on workshops. SPSS for Windows seminars will be offered in major U.S. and European cities on a regular basis. For more information on these seminars, call the SPSS Inc. Training Department toll-free at 1-800-543-6607.

Technical Support

The services of SPSS Technical Support are available to registered customers of SPSS for Windows. Customers may call Technical Support for assistance in using SPSS products or for installation help for one of the supported hardware environments.

To reach Technical Support, call 1-312-329-3410. Be prepared to identify yourself, your organization, and the serial number of your system.

If you are a Value Plus or Customer EXPress customer, use the priority 800 number that you received with your materials. For information on subscribing to the Value Plus or Customer EXPress plan, call SPSS Software Sales at 1-800-543-2185.

Additional Publications

Additional copies of SPSS product manuals may be purchased from Prentice Hall, the exclusive distributor of SPSS publications. To order, fill out and mail the Publications order form included with your system or call toll-free. If you represent a bookstore or have an account with Prentice Hall, call 1-800-223-1360. If you are not an account customer, call 1-800-374-1200. In Canada, call 1-800-567-3800. Outside of North America, contact your local Prentice Hall office.

Lend Us Your Thoughts

Your comments are important. So send us a letter and let us know about your experiences with SPSS products. We especially like to hear about new and interesting applications using the SPSS for Windows system. Write to SPSS Inc. Marketing Department, Attn: Micro Software Products Manager, 444 N. Michigan Avenue, Chicago IL, 60611.

Contents

1 A Quick Tour

This tour provides a quick preview of SPSS for Windows. More detailed information is available in later chapters and in the online Help system. The following techniques are briefly demonstrated:

- Starting and exiting from SPSS
- Opening a data file in the SPSS Data Editor
- Using the SPSS Statistics menu to obtain a frequency table and bar chart
- Viewing statistical output and charts
- Getting information from online Help and the online tutorial

This session will use the mouse. If you need information on using Windows or the mouse, see your Windows documentation.

The Online Tutorial

The SPSS online tutorial, installed along with the SPSS for Windows software, provides an overview of SPSS. While the online tutorial lacks the "hands on" approach of the tutorials in this manual, it provides a more complete introduction to a number of SPSS features, such as the toolbar. (Other topics, such as data transformations, are covered more extensively in the manual.)

To start the tutorial, double-click on the SPSS tutorial icon in the SPSS program group (shown in Figure 1.2). If SPSS is already running, you can start the tutorial by choosing SPSS Tutorial from the Help menu. The tutorial main menu is shown in Figure 1.1.

Figure 1.1 SPSS online tutorial main menu

If SPSS is already running, you can run the tutorial by selecting SPSS Tutorial from the Help menu.

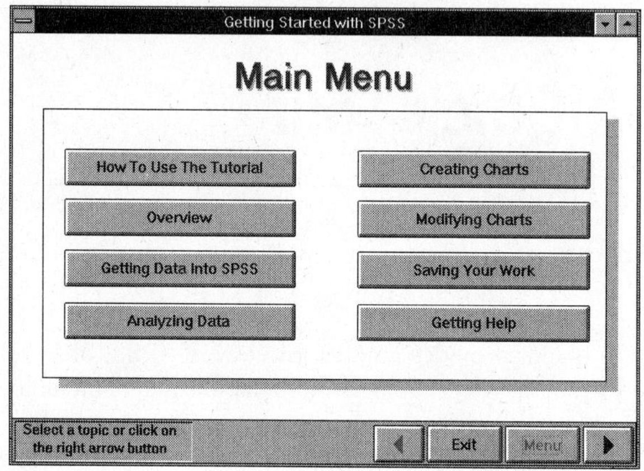

Select a topic, or click on the arrow button to go straight through the tutorial from beginning to end. Select Exit to leave the tutorial at any time.

Getting Started

The SPSS program group, created when you install SPSS, is shown in Figure 1.2.

Figure 1.2 SPSS program group

SPSS icon

SPSS

SPSS 6.1 SPSS Tutorial Setup

To start an SPSS session:

❶ Double-click with the mouse on the SPSS icon, or select the SPSS icon and press [↵Enter].

This opens the SPSS application window, an output window, and the Data Editor window, as shown in Figure 1.3.

Figure 1.3 SPSS application, output, and Data Editor windows

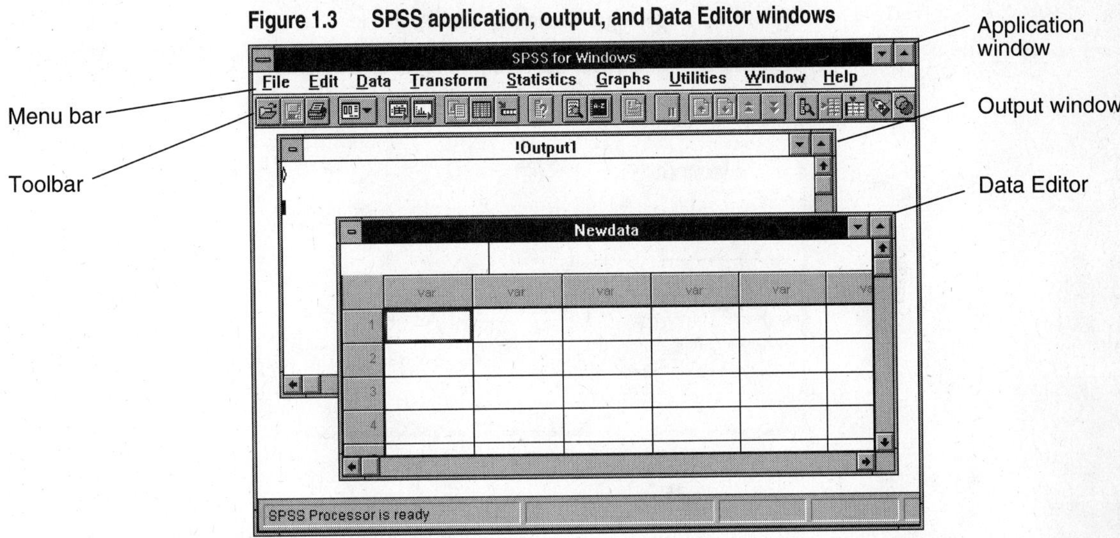

Opening a Data File

For this example, the data are in a file named *employee.sav* (See the Preface if you don't find this file on your system).

❶ Click on File on the menu bar.

This opens the File menu, which contains a list of options (New, Open, etc.).

❷ Click on Open ▸.

This opens a submenu, which lists various types of files. Data is the first type.

❸ Click on Data....

Throughout the rest of this book, the following shorthand will be used to indicate menu selections:

File
  Open ▸
    Data...

This sequence of steps opens the Open Data File dialog box, as shown in Figure 1.4.

Figure 1.4 Opening a previously saved data file

File Name box

List of files

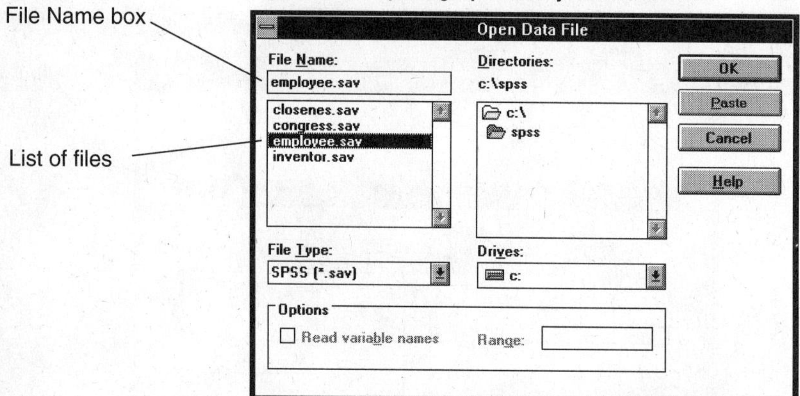

A File Name box is in the upper left corner, and below it is a list of files whose names end in *.sav.* One of the files is named *employee.sav.* (See the Preface if you don't find this file on your system. See Chapter 4 for more information about opening a data file.)

❹ Select *employee.sav* on the list.

This enters the name of the file in the File Name box.

Another way to open a file is to double-click on the filename on the list.

❺ Click on OK.

This opens the data file. The Data Editor window, containing data from *employee.sav*, is shown in Figure 1.5. If your data file displays words instead of numbers in the *gender* and *race* columns, open the Utilities menu and click on Value Labels.

Figure 1.5 Data Editor window

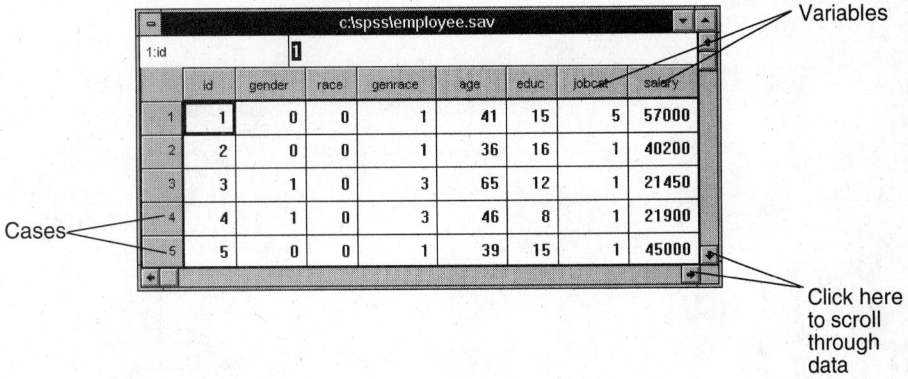

c:\spss\employee.sav

1:id 1

	id	gender	race	genrace	age	educ	jobcat	salary
1	1	0	0	1	41	15	5	57000
2	2	0	0	1	36	16	1	40200
3	3	1	0	3	65	12	1	21450
4	4	1	0	3	46	8	1	21900
5	5	0	0	1	39	15	1	45000

Variables

Cases

Click here to scroll through data

Some variables use numeric codes for categories. For the variable gender, 0 is a code for male and 1 is a code for female.

At the top of the data window is a row of names for the types of information included in the columns of the data file. These are called **variables**. The first variable, *id*, indicates that the numbers in the first column represent ID numbers for employees. At the right side of the window, the variable *salary* indicates that the column contains the annual salary for each employee.

The rows in the data file are called **cases**. In this file, each of 474 cases contains the data for one employee.

Calculating Simple Statistics

Now that data are available to SPSS, you can calculate some simple statistics. When you first start to analyze a set of data, you often want to know how many cases are in various categories. SPSS does the counting for you and displays the results in a table.

To see the names of the job categories, you can double-click on the variable jobcat at the top of the column and then click on Labels....

The variable *jobcat* contains codes for employee job categories. Each type of job is coded with a number between 1 and 5. A label for each of the code numbers is stored in the data file, and SPSS will use the labels when it displays the results.

❶ To calculate how many cases are in specified categories, from the menus choose:

Statistics
  Summarize ▶
    Frequencies...

Figure 1.6 shows the Statistics menu and Summarize submenu.

Figure 1.6 Choosing a statistical procedure

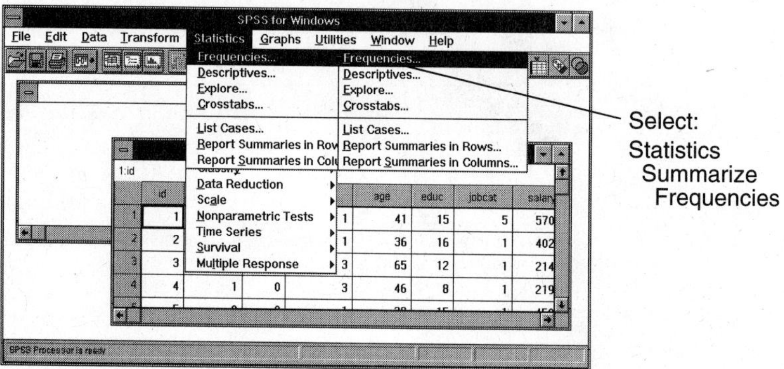

Choosing the Frequencies procedure from the menus opens the Frequencies dialog box, as shown in Figure 1.7. The Frequencies procedure counts the number of cases in various categories

Figure 1.7 Selecting variables

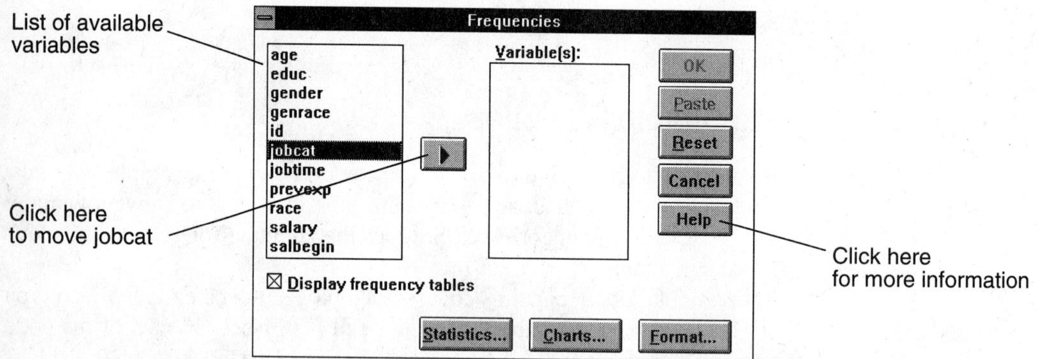

The variables available in the *employee.sav* data file are listed in the box on the left.

You can double-click on jobcat to move it to the Variable(s) list.

❷ Select *jobcat* and then click on [▸].

This moves *jobcat* to the Variable(s) list. At this point, what to do next may not be obvious. A quick source of information is the SPSS Help facility.

❸ Click on Help in the dialog box.

This opens a window containing information about the current dialog box, Frequencies, as shown in Figure 1.8. Several words within the Help text are highlighted, indicating links to additional information.

Figure 1.8 Frequencies Help

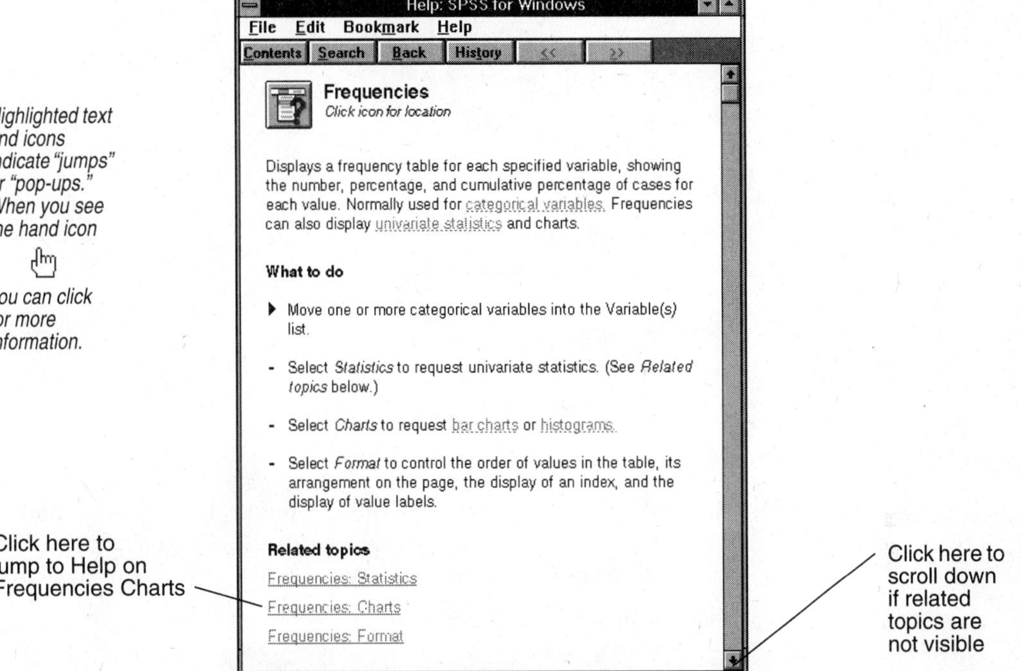

Under Related topics, click on Frequencies Charts.

This opens another Help window, which contains information about charts. It tells you that a bar chart is appropriate for a variable with few distinct values. (The variable *jobcat* is such a variable—it has only five distinct values.) This window has some additional highlighted words. For example, the term *nominal level* may be unfamiliar to you.

❹ To find out more about the term, click on nominal level.

A box pops up that contains a definition of the term *Nominal variables*. When you have read as much of the definition as you want to, click again, and the definition box disappears.

❺ To exit from the Help window, click on File on the Help window menu bar and then click on Exit.

This returns you to the Frequencies dialog box.

6. Click on Charts....

This opens the Frequencies Charts dialog box, as shown in Figure 1.9.

Figure 1.9 Selecting a chart type

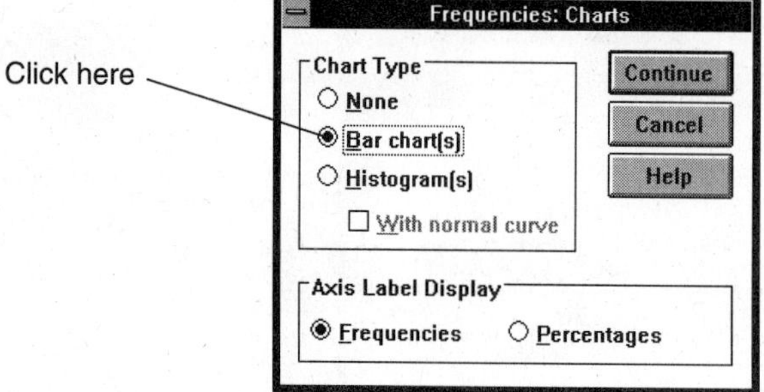

7. Select Bar chart(s).
8. Click on Continue.

This closes the Frequencies Charts dialog box.

9. In the Frequencies dialog box, click on OK.

The Frequencies dialog box closes and SPSS brings the output window to the foreground, where the bottom of a table is visible. An icon labeled Chart Carousel is displayed in the lower left corner, as shown in Figure 1.10.

Figure 1.10 Output window and Chart Carousel icon

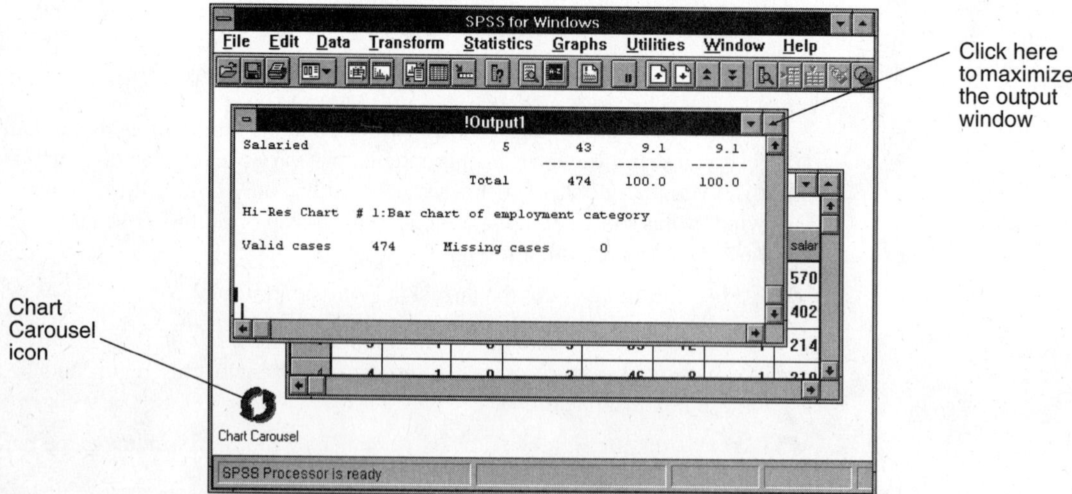

Viewing the Output

To see more of the table, you can maximize the output window.

❶ Click on ▲ in the upper right corner of the output window.

This increases its size, as shown in Figure 1.11. If you cannot see the whole table, you can scroll the window.

Figure 1.11 Table of frequencies

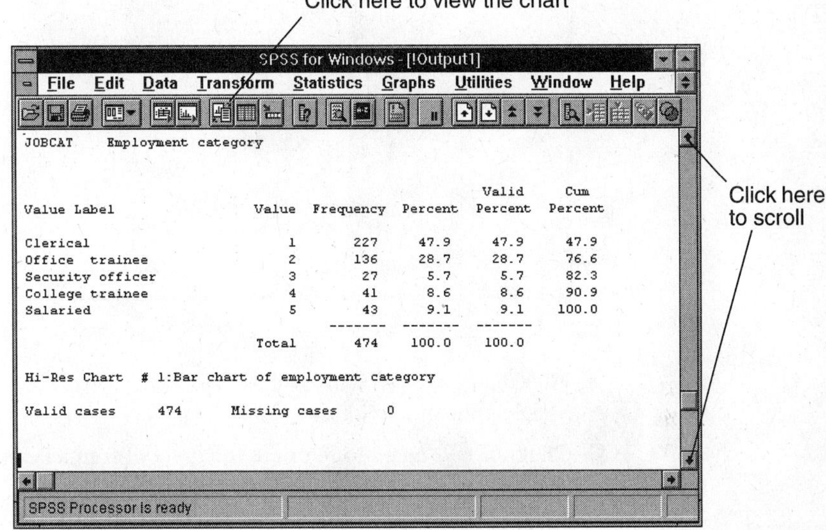

To find out more about terms such as Cum Percent, you can open the Glossary by clicking on .

The number of employees in each category is listed in the column labeled *Frequency*. There are 227 clerical workers, 136 office trainees, and so on. Percentages are listed in the next column.

❷ Click on [toolbar icon] on the toolbar.

This opens the Chart Carousel window, where you can see the bar chart of the job categories (see Figure 1.12).

Figure 1.12 Bar chart of job categories

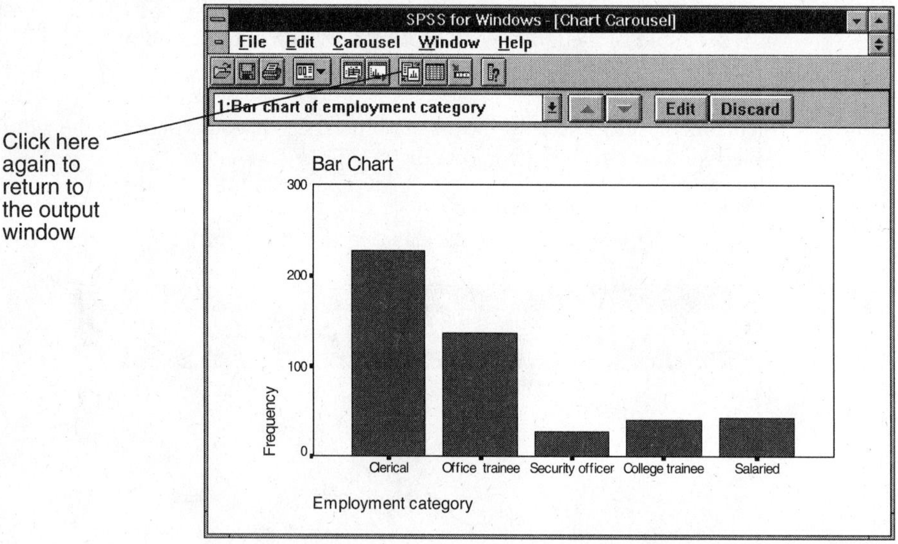

The Chart Carousel window has menus that are different from the menus in the SPSS application window.

❸ Click on [icon] again to return to the table of frequencies.

You can go back and forth between the frequency table and the chart as many times as you want.

Experimenting

If you want to try some other procedures, go ahead and experiment now. For example, you could try opening the Statistics menu and selecting Summarize ▸ and Descriptives.... After the dialog box opens, select the variables *age* and *salary*.

If you aren't sure how the descriptive statistics are defined, click on the Help pushbutton in the Descriptives dialog box and then on Options, one of the highlighted words. Then you can click on any statistic you don't recognize and a definition will pop up.

Click on OK in the Descriptives dialog box to run the Descriptives procedure.

Ending the SPSS Session

When you are ready to exit from SPSS, it asks if you want to save the contents of the Chart Carousel, output window, and data file. In this quick tour, you will exit without saving, as described below. For information on saving data files, see Chapter 3.

❶ To exit from SPSS, from the menus choose:

File
  Exit

as shown in Figure 1.13.

Figure 1.13 Exiting SPSS

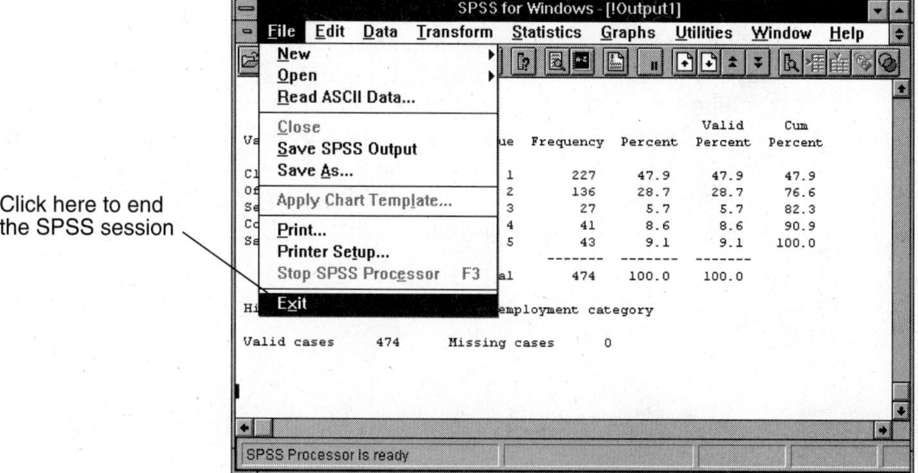

SPSS asks if you want to save the contents of the Chart Carousel.

❷ Click on No.

SPSS asks if you want to save the contents of the output window.

❸ Click on No.

This ends the SPSS session.

Should I Save the Data File?

If SPSS asks if you want to save the data file, click on No. This will happen only if you changed something in the data file, such as a data value, a variable name, or the order of the cases. When you use a file and see it in the Data Editor, the actual copy on the disk is not changed. The disk file is changed only if you save the file. Since the *employee.sav* file will be used in its original form in the next few chapters, it should not be changed.

What's Next?

The tutorials in the following chapters allow you to explore SPSS in greater depth, continuing the hands-on approach used in this quick tour. In addition, brief information on the basics of running selected statistical procedures is presented in the last section of this book. For detailed information on statistical procedures, consult a statistics or data analysis textbook.

The SPSS online tutorial provides a more complete introduction to a number of SPSS features such as the toolbar. (See "The Online Tutorial" on p. 1.)

For the most complete coverage of SPSS, consult the Online Help system. Chapter 2 provides an introduction to Help.

2 Tutorial: Using the Help System

SPSS for Windows uses the standard Windows Help system to provide information that you need for using SPSS and understanding the results. This tutorial demonstrates the following:

- Locating topics in the Help contents
- Navigating Help using "jumps" and "pop-ups"
- Searching the Help index for a specified topic

This tutorial can be done with any open data file (such as *employee.sav*), or it can be done with the Data Editor empty.

Locating Topics in the Help Contents

Suppose that you want to make a chart of your data. You have a picture in mind of what the chart should look like, but you are unsure of what it is called or whether it is available in SPSS. To find out, you can consult the Help system, as illustrated in the following steps.

You can also access Help by clicking on the Help button in any dialog box. Information about that dialog box will automatically be displayed.

❶ From the menus choose:

Help
  Contents

This opens the Help Contents window, as shown in Figure 2.1. (You can always return to this window from anywhere in SPSS Help by selecting the Contents button near the top of the Help window.)

Figure 2.1 Help system table of contents

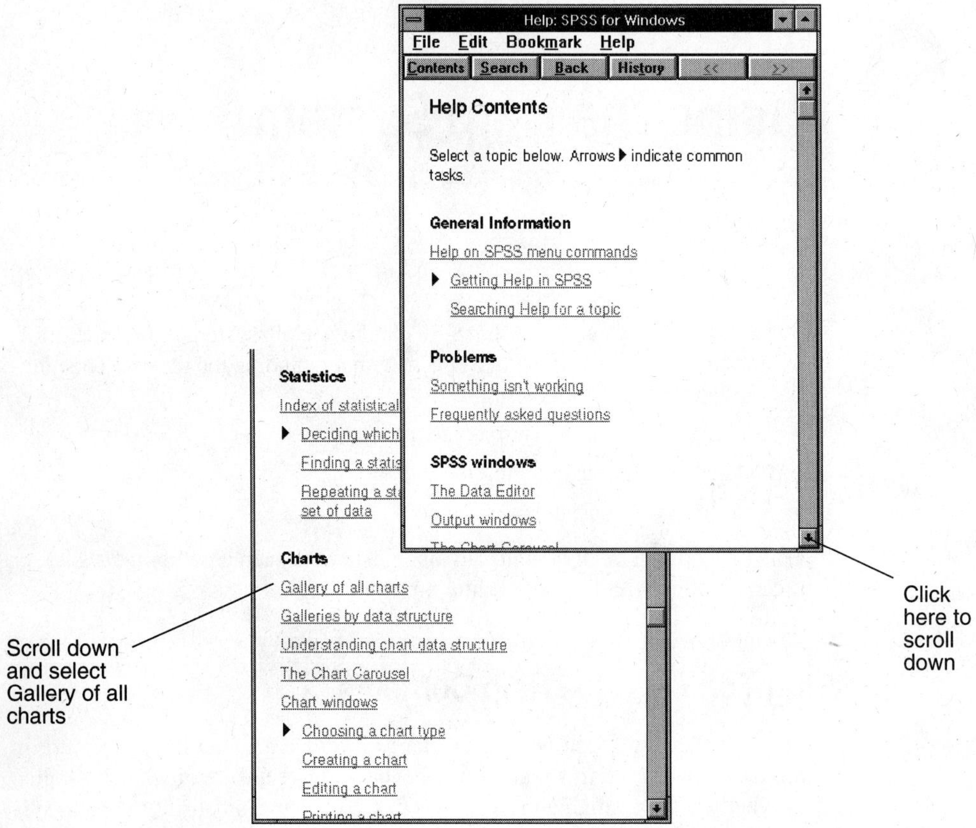

❷ Scroll down to the section on charts and select Gallery of all charts.

This “jumps” you to a window displaying icons for all of the chart types available in SPSS for Windows (see Figure 2.2).

Highlighted text and icons indicate “jumps” or “pop-ups.” When you see the hand icon you can click for more information.

Figure 2.2 Charts available in SPSS

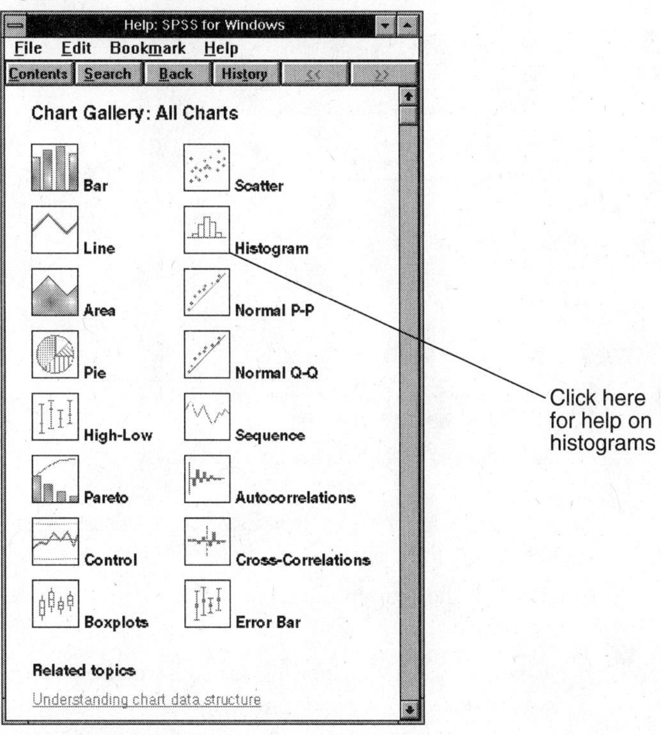

❸ Click on the histogram icon, as shown in Figure 2.2. (You may need to scroll to see this icon.)

This jumps you to a topic that describes the Histograms dialog box, as shown in Figure 2.3.

Figure 2.3 Information on histograms

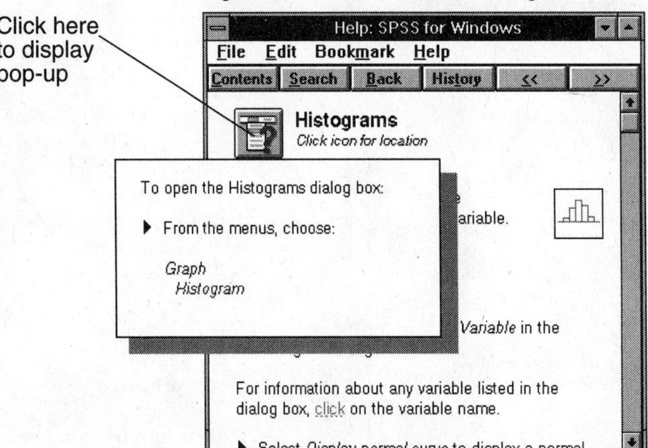

After reading the topic, if you decide to create a histogram, you need to know how to open the Histograms dialog box.

❹ Click on the icon in the upper left corner of the Help window, as shown in Figure 2.3.

A pop-up window displays instructions on how to open the Histograms dialog box. (Click the mouse or press any key to make the pop-up disappear.) When you have finished reading the information, you can exit from the Help window. In the next section, another way to access Help is illustrated.

❺ From the menu bar in the Help window, choose File and then choose Exit.

Searching

Rather than using the Help table of contents, you can often find the information you want more quickly by using Help's search feature. For example, suppose that you want to find out how to calculate percentiles and you do not find percentiles on the statistics menus.

❶ From the SPSS menus choose:

Help
 Search for Help on...

This opens the Search dialog box, as shown in Figure 2.4.

Figure 2.4 Search dialog box

Another way to open the Search dialog box is to click on the Search button in the Help window.

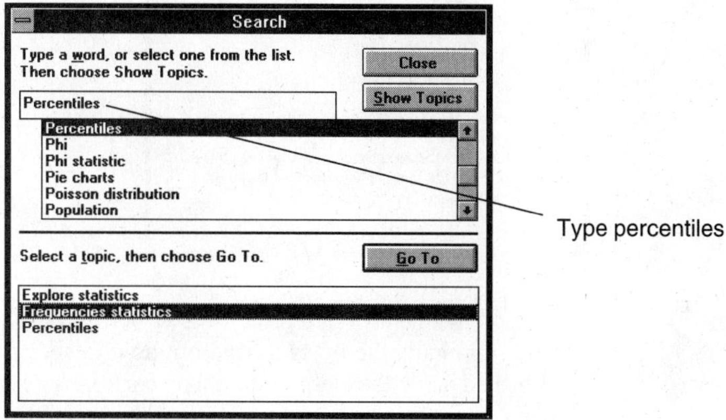

The window opens with the cursor in the text box.

❷ Type **percentiles** in the text box.

You can double-click on Percentiles on the list instead of clicking on the Show Topics pushbutton.

The list scrolls until Percentiles is highlighted.

❸ Click on Show Topics.

Several topics are listed.

❹ Select Frequencies statistics and then click on Go To.

This opens a Help window that gives you information about statistics available for the Frequencies procedure, as shown in Figure 2.5.

Figure 2.5 Information about Frequencies statistics

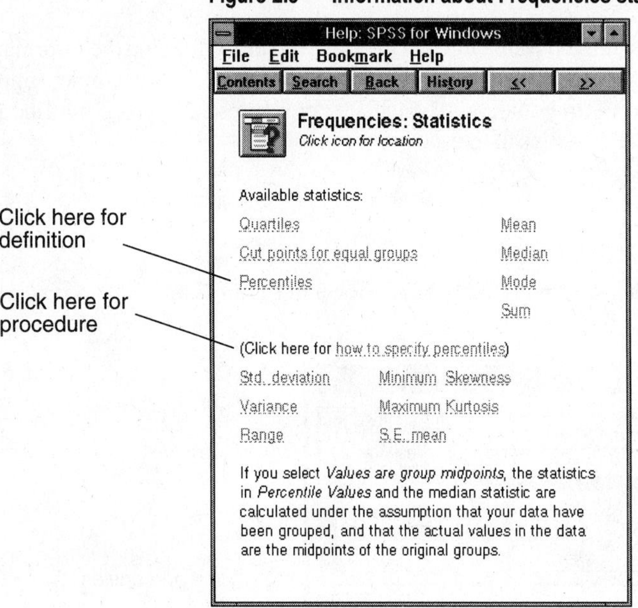

This window displays two references to percentiles. You can click on one for the definition and the other to find out how to specify percentiles. When you are finished using the Help system, you can return to where you were in SPSS. You may want to use the Frequencies procedure to calculate percentiles.

How to Ask for Help

Click on the Help button in any dialog box for information about that dialog box.

You can ask for help in any of the following ways:

- Click on the Help pushbutton in any dialog box for information about that dialog box.
- From the SPSS menu bar, open the Help menu and select a topic.
- Press F1 at any time in SPSS.
- For menu help, press ⇧Shift-F1 and then click on a menu option.
- For definitions of terms, select SPSS Glossary from the Help menu.

What's Next?

At this point, you can exit from SPSS. If you exit from SPSS and you have changed the data file in any way, you will be asked whether you want to save the changes. *Do not* save changes to the *employee.sav* data file.

If you want to try some more statistics, brief tutorials for selected procedures are provided in Chapter 12.

3 Tutorial: Using the Data Editor

This tutorial introduces the use of the Data Editor and demonstrates the following:

- Entering data in the Data Editor
- Naming variables
- Defining a string variable
- Defining value labels for a variable
- Saving data files

When you start an SPSS session, SPSS automatically opens an output window and the Data Editor window, as shown in Figure 3.1. (See Chapter 1 if you do not know how to start SPSS.)

Figure 3.1 SPSS application, Data Editor, and output windows

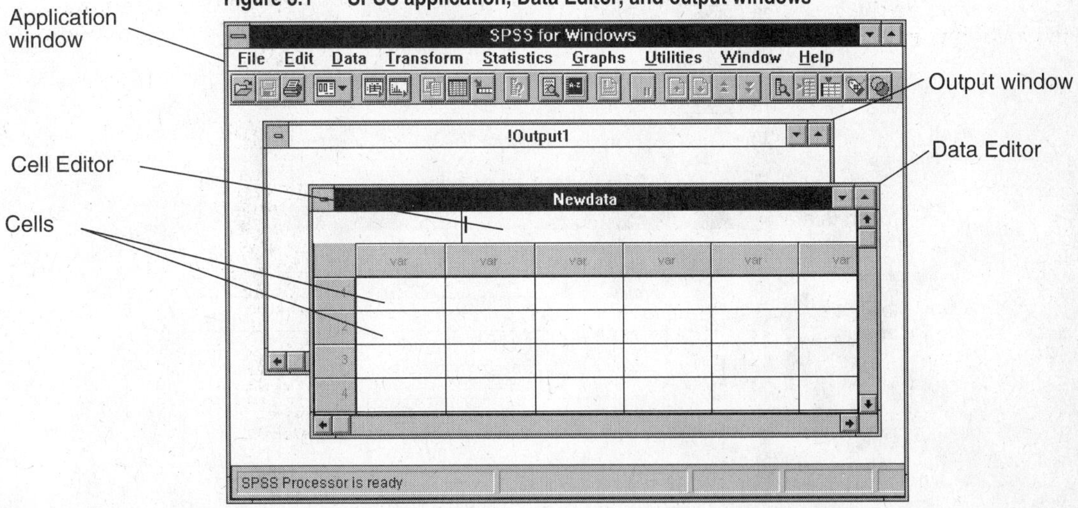

The Data Editor provides a convenient spreadsheet-like facility for entering, editing, and displaying the contents of your data file. You can use the Data Editor to enter data and create a data file. If you open a previously saved data file, you can use the Data Editor to change data values and add or delete cases and variables.

Entering Data

Entering numeric data (numbers) in the Data Editor is simple. For example, you could enter the age for the students in your class:

❶ Click on the first cell in the Data Editor (top left corner) and type:

21 [↵Enter]

The number appears in the cell editor at the top of the Data Editor as you enter it but is not displayed in the cell until you press [↵Enter].

By entering data in the cell, you automatically create a variable, and SPSS gives it the default name *var00001*, which is displayed at the top of the column. (Replacing default variable names is discussed on p. 23. Variable naming rules are listed on p. 28.)

❷ Continue entering values in the first column:

19 [↵Enter]

22 [↵Enter]

[↓] (skip this cell; do not enter a value)

22 [↵Enter]

20 [↵Enter]

19 [↵Enter]

The Data Editor should now look like Figure 3.2.

Figure 3.2 Data Editor after entering data

Newdata

	var00001	var	var	var	var	var
1	21.00					
2	19.00					
3	22.00					
4	.					
5	22.00					
6	20.00					
7	19.00					

Columns are variables

Rows are cases

Missing data value

A period is displayed in the cell that does not have a data value. The period represents the **system-missing value**. In this example, it could be a person in the class who did not want to reveal his or her age.

Naming Variables

The variable names NewVar, newvar, and NEWVAR are all identical in SPSS.

To replace the default variable name with a more descriptive variable name:

1. Double-click on the variable name *var00001* at the top of the first column in the Data Editor window, or select any cell in the first column and from the menus choose:

   Data
   Define Variable...

   This opens the Define Variable dialog box.

2. Delete the default variable name *var00001* and type **age** in the Variable Name text box.

3. Click on OK.

   This closes the Define Variable dialog box and changes the variable name to *age*, which is now displayed at the top of the first column in the Data Editor.

Defining Variables

Names, dates, and other non-numeric data must be defined before you can enter them. If you want to enter anything other than simple numbers, you need to tell SPSS what kind of non-numeric data you want to enter. With SPSS, you can also assign descriptive variable labels and value labels that make it easier to interpret your data, charts, and statistical results.

1. Click on the first cell in the second column of the Data Editor (to the right of the column of numbers you entered earlier).

2. Type **m** (or any other letter).

   SPSS does not accept the value, and your computer probably beeps at you. Since "m" is not a numeric value, you need to define the data type for SPSS before you can enter the value.

3. Double-click on the top of the second column (on the dimmed heading labeled var), or click on any cell in the second column, and from the menus choose:

   Data
   Define Variable...

   This opens the Define Variable dialog box, as shown in Figure 3.3.

Figure 3.3 Define Variable dialog box

Define Variable
Variable Name: gender
OK
Cancel
Help
Variable Description
Type: Numeric8.2
Variable Label:
Missing Values: None
Alignment: Right
Change Settings
Type...
Missing Values...
Labels..
Column Format...

Change variable name to gender

❹ Delete the default variable name *var00002* and type **gender** in the Variable Name text box.

❺ Click on Type... in the Change Settings group.

This opens the Define Variable Type dialog box, as shown in Figure 3.4.

Figure 3.4 Define Variable Type dialog box

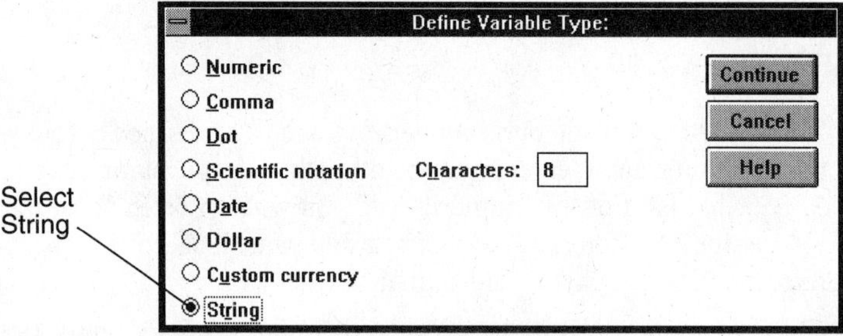

❻ Select String and then click on Continue to return to the Define Variable dialog box.

SPSS now knows that the variable *gender* is a string variable. A **string variable** can contain both letters and numbers.

❼ Click on Labels... in the Change Settings group at the bottom of the Define Variable dialog box.

This opens the Define Labels dialog box, as shown in Figure 3.5.

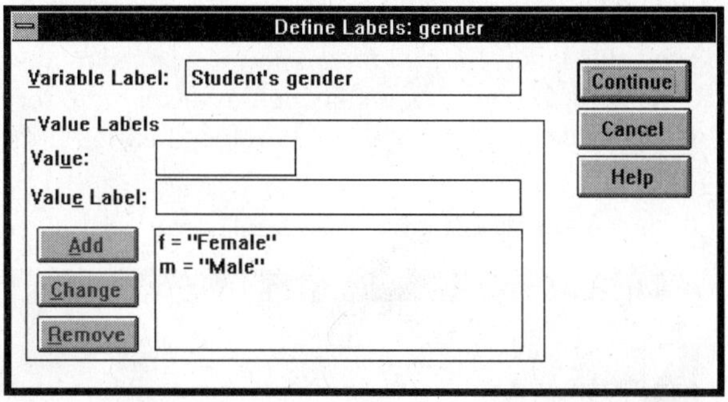

Value labels can be up to 60 characters long, but most SPSS procedures display only the first 20 characters.

Figure 3.5 Define Labels dialog box

8 Type **Student's gender** in the Variable Label text box.

This descriptive variable label will be displayed in statistical output and in charts that use the variable *gender.*

9 Type **m** in the Value text box.

10 Type **Male** in the Value Label text box.

11 Click on Add.

12 Go back and type **f** in the Value text box.

13 Type **Female** in the Value Label text box.

14 Click on Add, and then click on Continue to return to the Define Variable dialog box.

15 Click on OK to accept the variable definition and close the Define Variable dialog box.

String data values are case sensitive. A value label assigned to m will not be used for data entered as M.

You can now use the single letter codes **m** and **f** (lowercase in this example) for data entry, and SPSS will display the more descriptive value labels, *Male* and *Female*, in statistical output and charts.

16 In the Data Editor column for the string variable *gender*, type the following:

m [↵Enter]

m [↵Enter]

f [↵Enter]

m [↵Enter]

f [↵Enter]

f [↵Enter]

m [↵Enter]

You can also display value labels by clicking on  .

17 From the menus choose:

Utilities
 Value Labels

The value labels for *gender* are now displayed in the Data Editor, as shown in Figure 3.6. If you click on any cell in the column for the variable *gender*, the actual value will be displayed in the cell editor at the top of the Data Editor window.

You can open a window summarizing variable definition information by clicking on  .

Figure 3.6 Data Editor with value labels displayed

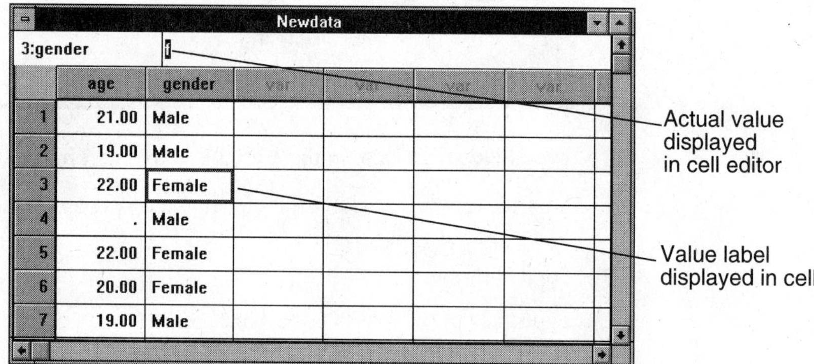

Saving a Data File

If you want to save the data file:

1. Make the Data Editor the active window (click anywhere in the Data Editor).
2. From the menus choose:

   File
    Save As...

   This opens the Save Data As dialog box, as shown in Figure 3.7.
3. Enter a name for the data file in the File Name text box and click on OK to save the data file in SPSS format.

Figure 3.7 Save Data As dialog box

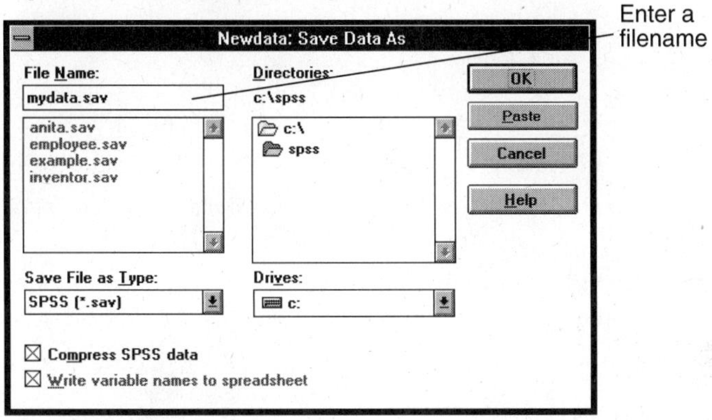

Enter a filename

To save to a floppy disk, select a: or b: from the drop-down Drives list.

By default, SPSS saves data files in SPSS format. For information on saving (or reading) data files in other formats, see Chapter 9.

Additional Information

The following sections provide additional information that you might find useful.

Missing Values

The data you want to use for analysis may not always contain complete information for every case. For example, some respondents may refuse to answer a certain survey question. SPSS provides two methods for handling missing values:

- **System-missing value**. If no value is entered for a numeric variable, SPSS assigns the system-missing value (represented by a period in the Data Editor).
- **User-missing values**. Data can be missing for a variety of reasons. If you know why particular data are missing, you can assign values that identify information missing for specific reasons and then instruct SPSS to flag these values as missing. To define user-missing values, use the Define Variable option on the Data menu, and select Missing Values in the Define Variable dialog box.

Variable Naming Rules

The basic rules for SPSS variable names are:

- The name must begin with a letter.
- Variable names cannot end with a period.
- The length of the variable name cannot exceed eight characters.
- Variable names cannot contain blanks or special characters (for example, !, ?, ', and *).
- Each variable name must be unique. Duplication is not allowed.
- Variable names are not case sensitive.

What's Next?

At this point, you can exit from SPSS or continue with the next tutorial.

4 Tutorial: Working with Statistics and Output

This tutorial introduces the use of the SPSS Statistics menu and output window and demonstrates the following:

- Opening a data file in the SPSS Data Editor
- Obtaining a crosstabulation of two variables
- Navigating, editing, and saving SPSS output

Opening an SPSS Data File

SPSS for Windows is able to open a number of different types of data files, including spreadsheet files created with Lotus 1-2-3, Excel, and Multiplan; dBASE files; and tab-delimited ASCII files. For more information about how to open different types of data files, see Chapter 9.

This tutorial uses the data file *employee.sav* (See the Preface if you don't find this file on your system).

❶ To open the *employee.sav* data file, from the menus choose:

File
  Open ▸
    Data...

This opens the Open Data File dialog box, as shown in Figure 4.1.

Figure 4.1 Open Data File dialog box

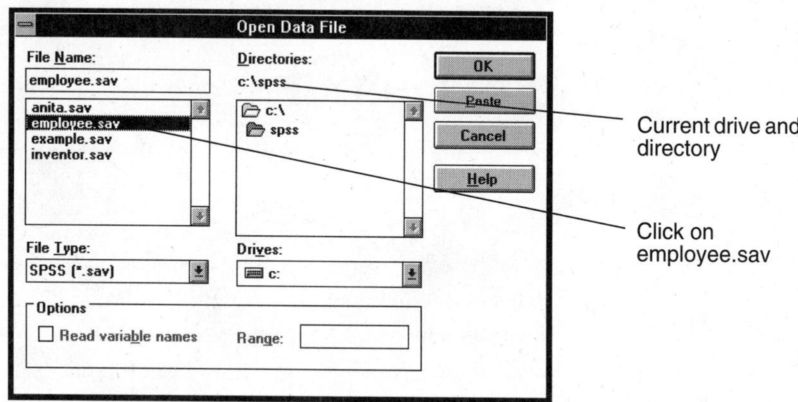

If you cannot find the data file, be sure you are looking in the directory where SPSS is installed (usually c:\spss) and that files with the .sav extension are listed.

❷ Select *employee.sav* on the list of files.

❸ Click on OK or press [↵Enter].

The data file is displayed in the Data Editor window, as shown in Figure 4.2. The appearance of the data file varies depending on whether or not value labels are displayed.

Figure 4.2 Data Editor windows (with and without value labels displayed)

You can display (or hide) value labels by clicking on [button].

c:\spss\employee.sav

1:gender 0

	id	gender	race	genrace	age	educ	jobcat	salary
1	1	0	0	1	41	15	5	5700
2	2	0	0	1	36	16	1	4020
3	3	1	0	3	65	12	1	2145
4								
5								

c:\spss\employee.sav

1:gender 0

	id	gender	race	genrace	age	educ	jobcat
1	1	Male	White	White males	41	15	Salaried
2	2	Male	White	White males	36	16	Clerical
3	3	Female	White	White females	65	12	Clerical
4	4	Female	White	White females	46	8	Clerical
5	5	Male	White	White males	39	15	Clerical

Value

Value label

The Employee Data File

Variables such as gender and jobcat use numeric codes to represent categorical information.

Variables such as age and salary represent actual numerical data.

The file *employee.sav* contains historical data on employees for a company. The data were gathered as part of a study to determine whether the company had discriminated against women and minorities in its employment practices. The file contains the following variables:

- *id*—the employee's identification number (in order of hiring).
- *gender*—coded as follows: 0=male, 1=female.
- *race*—the employee's minority status: 0=white, 1=minority.
- *genrace*—combines information about gender and minority status into a single code: 1=white males, 2=minority males, 3=white females, 4=minority females.
- *age*—the age of the employee.
- *educ*—the highest grade level completed by the employee: 12=high school diploma, 16=bachelor's degree, and so on.
- *jobcat*—the individual's employment category: 1=clerical, 2=office trainee, 3=security officer, 4=college trainee, 5=salaried.
- *salary*—the employee's current salary, adjusted to 1992 dollars.
- *salbegin*—the employee's salary at time of hiring, in 1992 dollars.
- *jobtime*—the number of months the employee has been with the company.
- *prevexp*—employee's experience (in months) prior to joining the company.

Using Statistical Procedures

The Statistics menu contains a list of general statistical categories. The arrow (▶) following each menu selection indicates that there is an additional menu level. The individual statistical procedures are listed at this submenu level.

To examine the relationship between job category, gender, and race among company employees, you can crosstabulate the variables *jobcat* and *genrace*.

❶ To obtain a crosstabulation, from the menus choose:

Statistics
  Summarize ▶
    Crosstabs...

You can directly access variable information from any dialog box. Simply click on any variable with the right mouse button.

This opens the Crosstabs dialog box, as shown in Figure 4.3.

Figure 4.3 Crosstabs dialog box

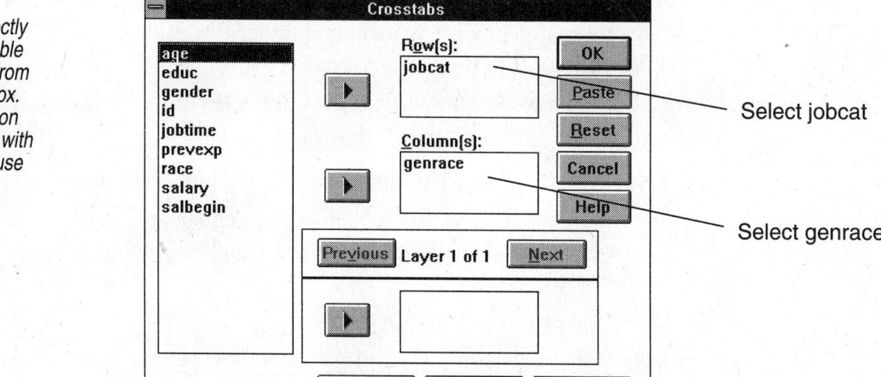

❷ Select *jobcat* on the variable list and click on the ▶ pushbutton next to the Row(s) list box.

This moves *jobcat* to the Row(s) list.

❸ Select *genrace* on the variable list and click on the ▶ pushbutton next to the Column(s) list box.

This moves *genrace* to the Column(s) list. The dialog box should appear as shown in Figure 4.3 above.

❹ Click on OK.

This closes the dialog box and runs the procedure.

The results—a crosstabulation for *jobcat* and *genrace*—are displayed in the output window, as shown in Figure 4.4.

Figure 4.4 Crosstabulation displayed in output window

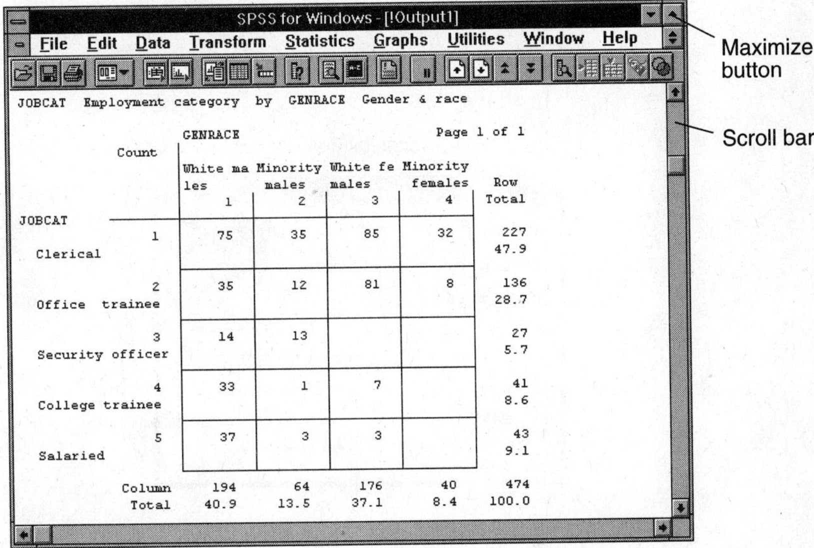

JOBCAT Employment category by GENRACE Gender & race

GENRACE Page 1 of 1

Count	White males 1	Minority males 2	White females 3	Minority females 4	Row Total
JOBCAT					
1 Clerical	75	35	85	32	227 47.9
2 Office trainee	35	12	81	8	136 28.7
3 Security officer	14	13			27 5.7
4 College trainee	33	1	7		41 8.6
5 Salaried	37	3	3		43 9.1
Column Total	194 40.9	64 13.5	176 37.1	40 8.4	474 100.0

You can use the maximize button and scroll bars to see more of the output.

Running Procedures with Additional Specifications

In running a procedure in SPSS, you can request additional specifications in subdialog boxes, which are accessed from the main dialog box.

In the output from the above crosstabulation, the distribution of gender and race does not appear to be equal across different job categories. Most women (and *all* minority women) are either clerical workers or office trainees, while a large majority of salaried employees are white males. This suggests that there is a relationship between the variables *genrace* and *jobcat*. But what is this relationship? And is it statistically significant?

To more closely examine the distribution of *genrace* across each value of *jobcat*, you can repeat the above crosstabulation, using an additional specification to display expected counts in each cell.

❶ To obtain a crosstabulation with expected counts displayed in each cell, from the menus choose:

Statistics
  Summarize ▸
    Crosstabs...

You can also reopen the dialog box by clicking on .

This reopens the Crosstabs dialog box, as shown in Figure 4.3 on p. 32. (Note that SPSS "remembers" your previous selections.)

❷ Move the variable *jobcat* to the Row(s) list if it is not already there.

❸ Move *genrace* to the Column(s) list if it is not already there.

❹ Click on Cells... in the Crosstabs dialog box.

This opens the Crosstabs Cell Display dialog box, as shown in Figure 4.5.

Figure 4.5 Crosstabs Cell Display dialog box

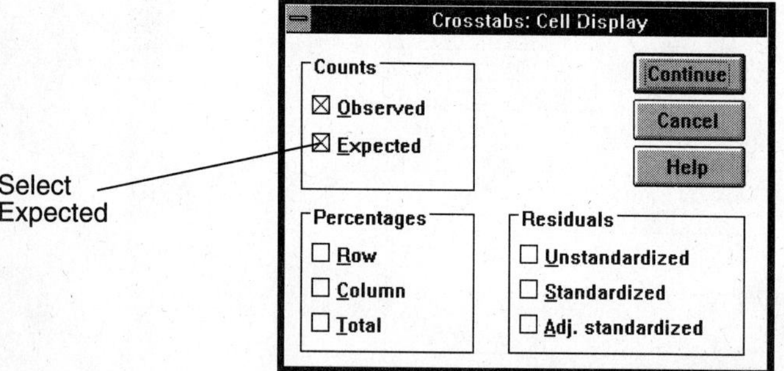

❺ Click on Expected in the Counts group.

Expected counts will be displayed in each cell of the crosstabulation. The **expected count** is the number of observations that would occur in each cell if there were no relationship between the two variables.

❻ Click on Continue to close the Crosstabs Cell Display dialog box and return to the main Crosstabs dialog box.

❼ Click on OK to run the procedure.

The results are displayed in the output window, as shown in Figure 4.6.

Figure 4.6 Crosstabulation with expected percentages

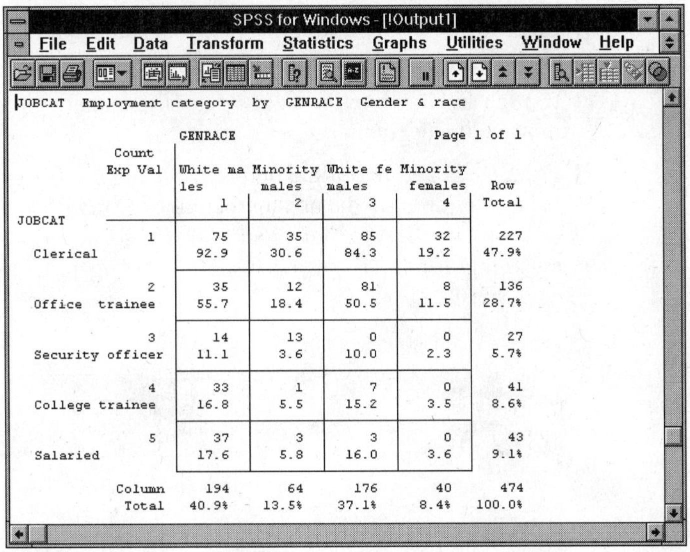

SPSS for Windows - [!Output1]

File Edit Data Transform Statistics Graphs Utilities Window Help

JOBCAT Employment category by GENRACE Gender & race

GENRACE Page 1 of 1

Count / Exp Val	White males 1	Minority males 2	White females 3	Minority females 4	Row Total
JOBCAT					
1 Clerical	75 92.9	35 30.6	85 84.3	32 19.2	227 47.9%
2 Office trainee	35 55.7	12 18.4	81 50.5	8 11.5	136 28.7%
3 Security officer	14 11.1	13 3.6	0 10.0	0 2.3	27 5.7%
4 College trainee	33 16.8	1 5.5	7 15.2	0 3.5	41 8.6%
5 Salaried	37 17.6	3 5.8	3 16.0	0 3.6	43 9.1%
Column Total	194 40.9%	64 13.5%	176 37.1%	40 8.4%	474 100.0%

The expected cell counts provide further indication that jobs may be unequally distributed across gender and race categories. For example, there are more than twice as many white males in salaried positions as you would expect if the two variables were unrelated. The actual count is 37, while the expected count is only 17.6. Conversely, the expected number of black females in clerical jobs is only 19.2, while the actual number is 32, 67% more than you would expect if the two variables were independent of each other.

While the above crosstabulation suggests that a relationship does indeed exist between *genrace* and *jobcat*, this analysis falls short of demonstrating that it is statistically significant.

Working with Output

Data analysis frequently requires numerous preliminary, exploratory steps, and many statistical procedures can generate a large volume of output. SPSS provides a number of facilities to help you navigate, edit, and save your results.

Navigating and Editing in the Output Window

To examine and modify your output:

1. Click anywhere in the output window to make it the active window. (You might also want to maximize the output window so that more of the output is visible.)
2. Use the scroll bar on the right side of the output window or press Ctrl-Home to move to the beginning of the output.
3. From the beginning of the output, click on ⊻ on the toolbar, and note how the cursor jumps to the next output block marker (each procedure you run generates a separate output block). If the second of the two crosstabulations (shown in Figure 4.7) is not visible, click again on the same tool until it becomes visible.

Figure 4.7 Output window

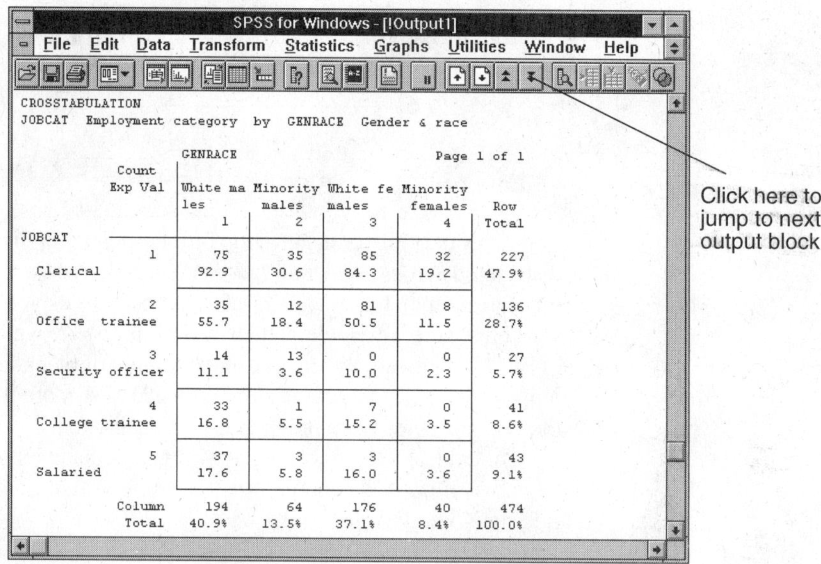

You can use the following tools to navigate through your output:

Select Search for Text from the Edit menu to locate a specific string of output.

4. Type the heading **CROSSTABULATION** at the top of the table (above the current heading), as shown in Figure 4.7.

❺ Click and drag the *right* mouse button to highlight the *Row Total* column, as shown in Figure 4.8.

Use the right mouse button to select rectangular blocks of text as shown here.

Use the left mouse button to select complete lines of text, as in Figure 4.9 on the following page.

Figure 4.8 Text column highlighted using click-and-drag with right mouse button

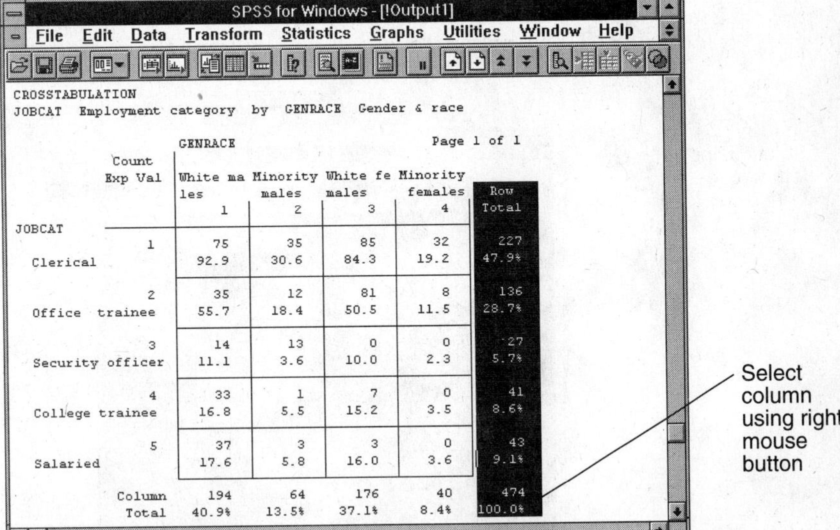

❻ Press Del to delete the highlighted column. (The row totals are not relevant to the question being explored in this analysis.)

Saving Output

Your SPSS output can be saved in a text file. You can save the entire contents of the output window or select and save only part of the output.

To select and save your second crosstabulation:

❶ Use the *left* mouse button to highlight the entire table, including the headings, as shown in Figure 4.9.

Figure 4.9 Text highlighted using click-and-drag with left mouse button

Select using left mouse button

SPSS for Windows - [!Output1]

File Edit Data Transform Statistics Graphs Utilities Window Help

CROSSTABULATION
JOBCAT Employment category by GENRACE Gender & race

Count Exp Val	GENRACE White males 1	Minority males 2	White females 3	Page 1 of 1 Minority females 4
JOBCAT				
1 Clerical	75 92.9	35 30.6	85 84.3	32 19.2
2 Office trainee	35 55.7	12 18.4	81 50.5	8 11.5
3 Security officer	14 11.1	13 3.6	0 10.0	0 2.3
4 College trainee	33 16.8	1 5.5	7 15.2	0 3.5
5 Salaried	37 17.6	3 5.8	3 16.0	0 3.6
Column Total	194 40.9%	64 13.5%	176 37.1%	40 8.4%

❷ From the menus choose:

File
  Save As...

This opens the Save SPSS Output As dialog box, as shown in Figure 4.10.

Figure 4.10 Save SPSS Output As dialog box

SPSS adds the extension .lst to output filenames, unless a different extension is typed.

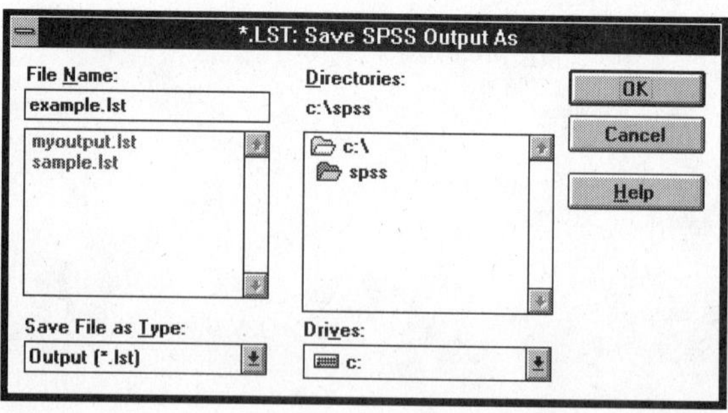

❸ Type a name for the file and click on OK.

A dialog box will be displayed asking whether you want to save the selected area only.

4. Click on Yes to save only the selected table, or click on No to save the entire contents of the output window.

Pasting Output into Another Application

You can paste your output into another Windows application, such as a word processing program. You can do this using any of the following three methods, all of which use the Windows clipboard:

- Highlight the output in the SPSS output window and choose Copy from the Edit menu to copy the output to the clipboard. In the target application, use the Paste Special option on the Edit menu to paste the output as a picture. This is probably the simplest method, but it will not be possible to edit the output in the target application.
- In SPSS, copy the output to the clipboard as above. In the target application, use Paste to paste the output as text. Generally, you will then need to apply a fixed-pitch font such as Courier or Courier New to the output so that spaces and tables align properly.
- In SPSS, choose Copy Table from the Edit menu to copy the output to the clipboard, and use Paste to paste the output into the target application. This option works only for text aligned in columns.

For more information on pasting output to other applications, see the "How do I..." topic in the online Help.

Finding Information about Variables

SPSS provides several ways to easily keep track of variable definition information:

- In most SPSS dialog boxes, click on any listed variable name with the *right* mouse button to pop up a window displaying any variable and value labels defined for that variable.
- For complete information about all of the variables in the current data file, select Variables from the Utilities menu. This opens the Variables window, as shown in Figure 4.11. For further instructions, click on Help in the Variables window.

You can also open the Variables window by clicking on .

Figure 4.11 Variables window

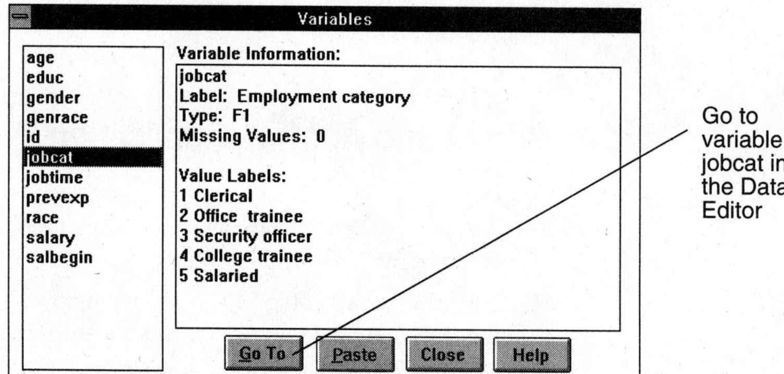

What's Next?

At this point, you can exit from SPSS or continue with the next tutorial. If you exit from SPSS and you have changed the data file in any way, you will be asked whether you want to save the changes. *Do not* save changes to the *employee.sav* data file.

5 Tutorial: Creating Bar Charts

This tutorial introduces the basics of creating charts using the SPSS Graphs menu and demonstrates the following:

- Creating a simple bar chart summarizing groups of cases
- Creating a simple bar chart summarizing separate variables
- Creating a clustered bar chart

This tutorial uses the file *employee.sav*, described in previous chapters. If you need help in opening the file, see Chapter 4.

Creating a Chart Summarizing Groups of Cases

Figure 5.1 shows a simple bar chart that plots the mean salary for employees within each job category.

Figure 5.1 Simple bar chart

A single categorical variable (jobcat) is summarized. Each bar represents the mean salary for a group of cases.

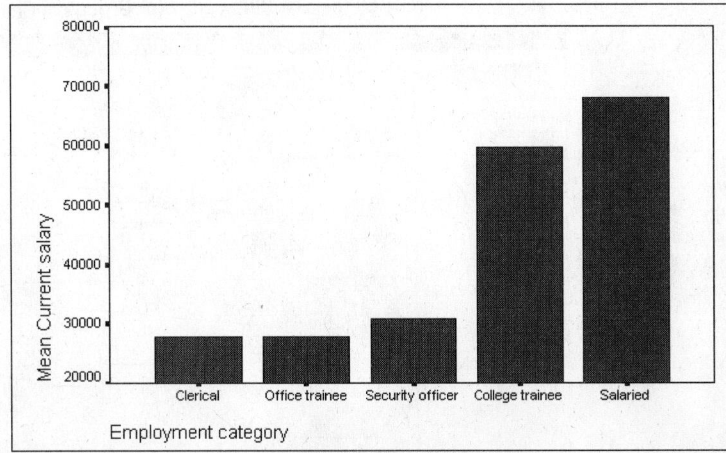

❶ To create the above bar chart, from the menus choose:

Graphs
 Bar...

This opens the Bar Charts dialog box, as shown in Figure 5.2.

Figure 5.2 Bar Charts dialog box

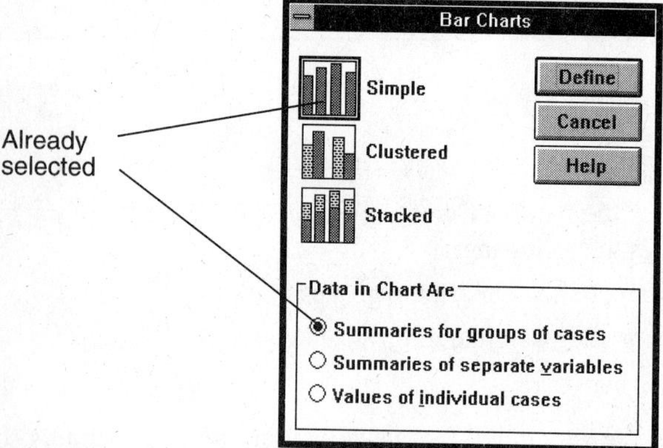

The option for a simple bar chart should already be selected, as well as the option Summaries for groups of cases, which is used to summarize a variable within categories.

❷ Click on Define.

This opens the Define Simple Bar Summaries for Groups of Cases dialog box, as shown in Figure 5.3.

Figure 5.3 Define Simple Bar Summaries for Groups of Cases dialog box

Each bar will represent the mean salary within a single job category.

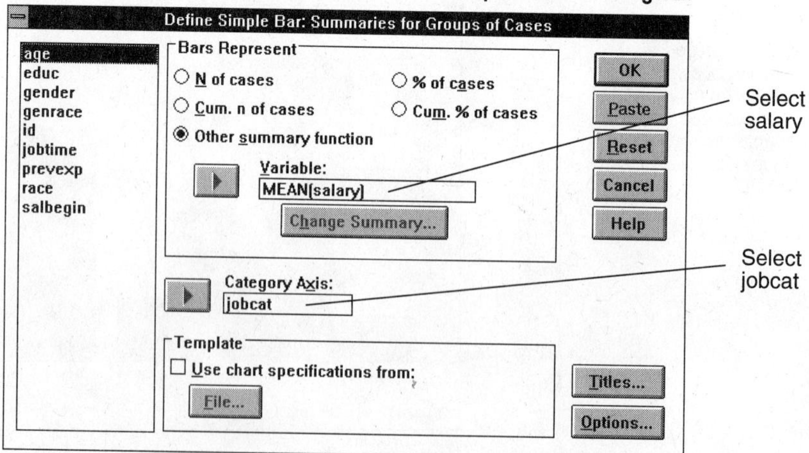

3. In the Bars Represent group, select Other summary function. Select *salary* for the summary function variable.

   MEAN(salary) appears in the Variable box.

4. Select *jobcat* for Category Axis.

   There will be a separate bar for each job category.

5. Click on OK.

   The chart is displayed in the Chart Carousel, as shown in Figure 5.4. Notice that the Chart Carousel menu bar and toolbar are now displayed.

Figure 5.4 Simple bar chart in the Chart Carousel

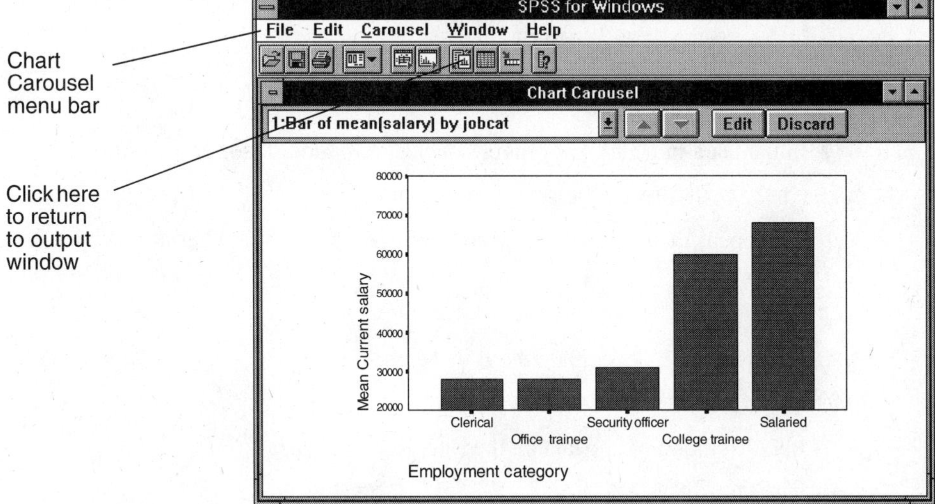

6. Click on [toolbar button] on the toolbar to activate the output window and restore the regular menu bar.

Creating a Chart Summarizing Separate Variables

Suppose you now want to compare beginning and current salaries. You can create a bar chart that shows mean current and beginning salaries for all employees.

1. From the menus choose:

   Graphs
   Bar...

This opens the Bar Charts dialog box, as shown in Figure 5.5.

Figure 5.5 Bar Charts dialog box

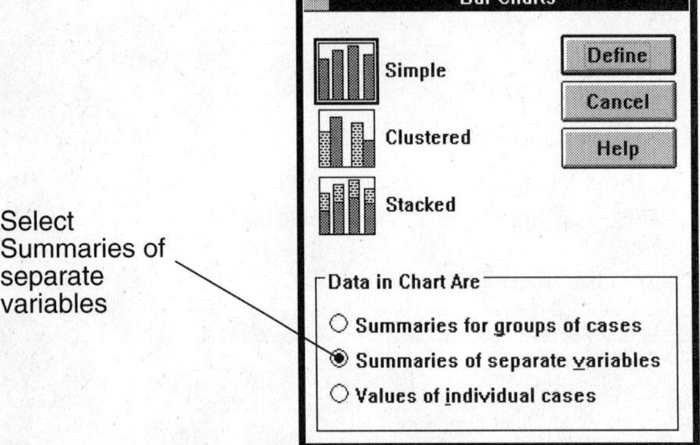

2. In the Data in Chart Are group, select Summaries of separate variables.
3. Click on Define.

   This opens the Define Simple Bar Summaries of Separate Variables dialog box, as shown in Figure 5.6.

4. Select *salary* on the variable list and click on [▶].

   MEAN(salary) appears on the Bars Represent list.

5. Select *salbegin* and click on [▶] again.

   MEAN(salbegin) appears on the Bars Represent list.

6. Click on OK.

SPSS displays the chart in the Chart Carousel (see Figure 5.7), which now holds both of the bar charts you created.

Figure 5.6 Define Simple Bar Summaries of Separate Variables dialog box

Each bar will represent the mean of a separate variable, across all cases.

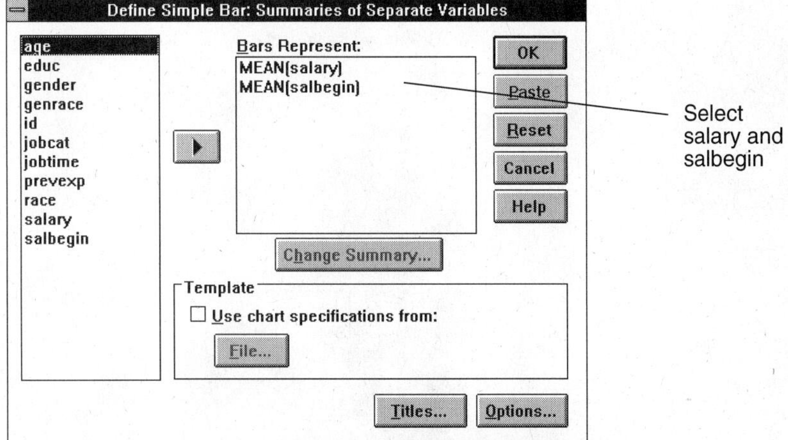

Figure 5.7 Bar chart of salary and salbegin in the Chart Carousel

Each bar represents the mean of a separate variable.

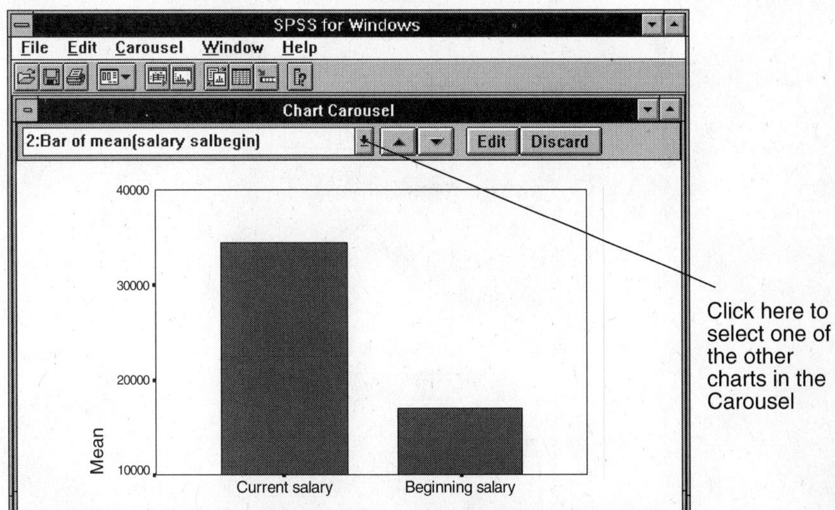

Creating a Clustered Bar Chart

In a clustered bar chart, there is a cluster of bars (rather than a single bar) for each point on the category axis. Figure 5.8 shows a clustered bar chart that plots the number of males and females within each job category.

There is a cluster of bars for each point on the category axis.

Figure 5.8 Clustered bar chart

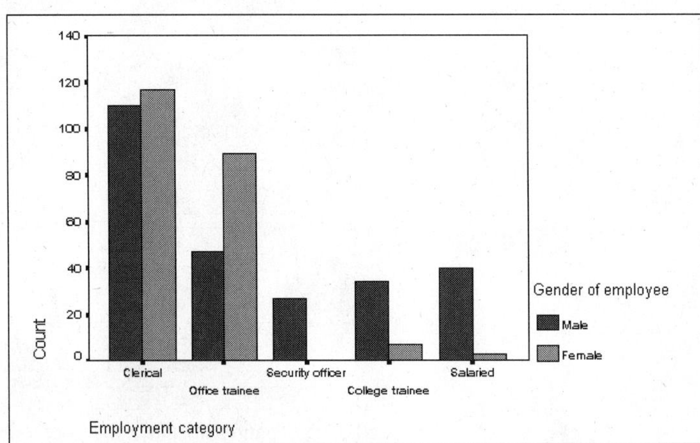

To create the above bar chart:

You can also use the Window menu to activate the output window.

❶ Click on [toolbar icon] on the toolbar.

This activates the output window and restores the regular SPSS menu bar.

❷ From the menus choose:

Graphs
  Bar...

This opens the Bar Charts dialog box, as shown in Figure 5.9.

Figure 5.9 Bar Charts dialog box

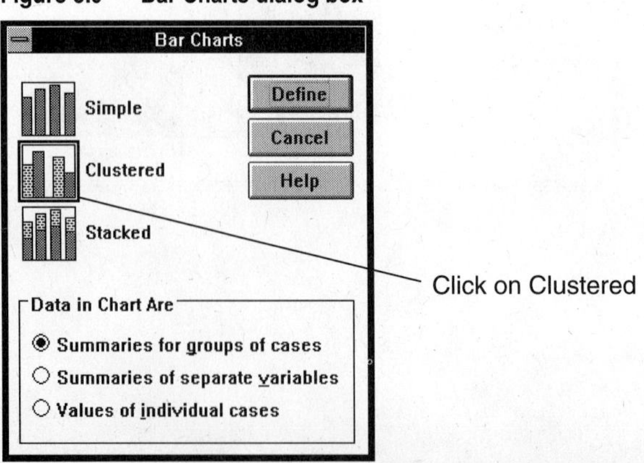

❸ To create a clustered bar chart, click on Clustered.

❹ In the Data in Chart Are group, select Summaries for groups of cases.

In this example, cases are first grouped according to job category and then further grouped within each job category according to gender.

❺ Click on Define.

This opens the Define Clustered Bar Summaries for Groups of Cases dialog box, as shown in Figure 5.10.

Figure 5.10 Define Clustered Bar Summaries for Groups of Cases dialog box

Categories of gender will be summarized within categories of jobcat.

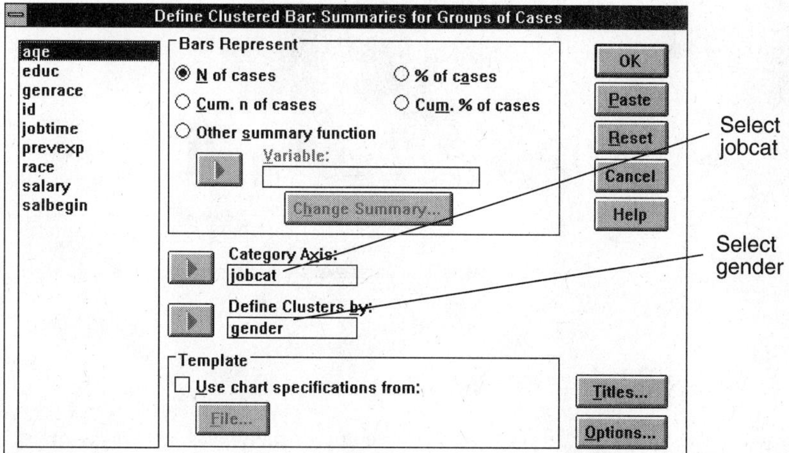

In the Bars Represent group, the default N of cases will chart the number of cases in each of the categories.

❻ Select *jobcat* for Category Axis.

There will be a separate cluster of bars for each job category.

❼ Select *gender* for Define Clusters by.

Within each cluster, there will be a separate bar for males and females.

❽ Click on OK.

Figure 5.11 shows the resulting chart.

Figure 5.11 Clustered bar chart in the Chart Carousel

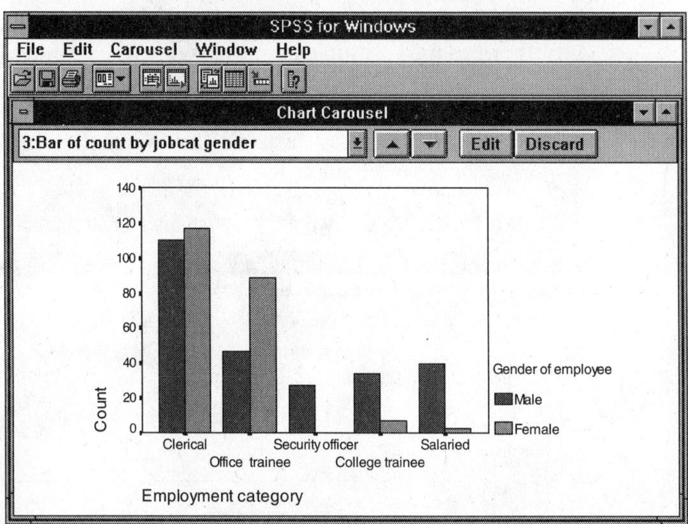

Saving the Charts

You can also save the chart by clicking on .

If you want to save any of the charts, select the chart in the Chart Carousel.

1. With the chart displayed in the Chart Carousel, from the menus choose:

   File
     Save As...

This opens the Save SPSS Chart As dialog box, as shown in Figure 5.12.

SPSS adds the extension .cht to chart filenames, unless another extension is typed.

Figure 5.12 Save SPSS Chart As dialog box

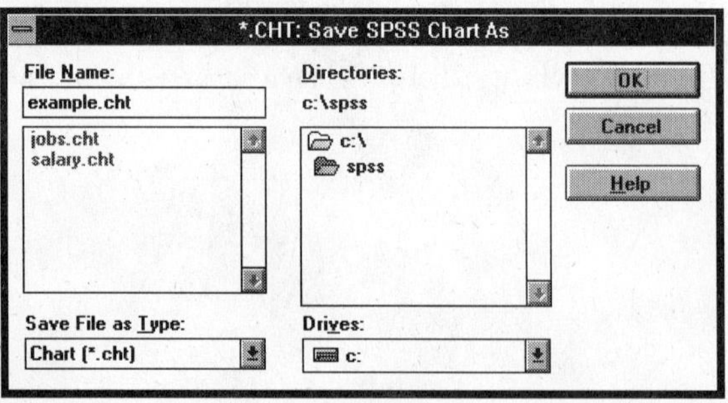

2. Enter a name for the chart and click on OK.

Pasting Charts into Another Application

To copy and paste a chart into another application, such as a word processing program:

1. Make the window containing the chart you want to copy the active window (click anywhere in the window).

2. From the menus choose:

   Edit
   Copy Chart

   This copies the chart to the Windows clipboard in metafile format.

3. Position the cursor in the target application where you want to place the chart.

4. From the target application's menus choose:

   Edit
   Paste Special...

5. From the Paste Special dialog box, select Picture.

What's Next?

At this point, you can choose to continue experimenting with the Graphs menu, continue with the next tutorial (where you will learn how to edit charts), or exit from SPSS. If you exit from SPSS, be sure that you *do not* save any changes to the *employee.sav* data file.

6 Tutorial: Creating and Modifying a Scatterplot

This tutorial introduces the basics of editing charts in a chart window and demonstrates the following:

- Creating a scatterplot
- Moving the scatterplot from the Chart Carousel into a chart window
- Using point selection mode to identify points in the scatterplot
- Changing the scale of the x-axis
- Adding a regression line and title to the scatterplot

This tutorial uses the file *employee.sav*, described in previous chapters. If you need help in opening the file, see Chapter 4.

Creating a Scatterplot

A scatterplot shows the relationship between two continuous variables, such as *salary* and *salbegin*.

❶ To create a scatterplot that shows the relationship between beginning and current salary, from the menus choose:

Graphs
 Scatter...

This opens the Scatterplot dialog box, as shown in Figure 6.1. (The Simple chart type is selected by default).

Figure 6.1 Scatterplot dialog box

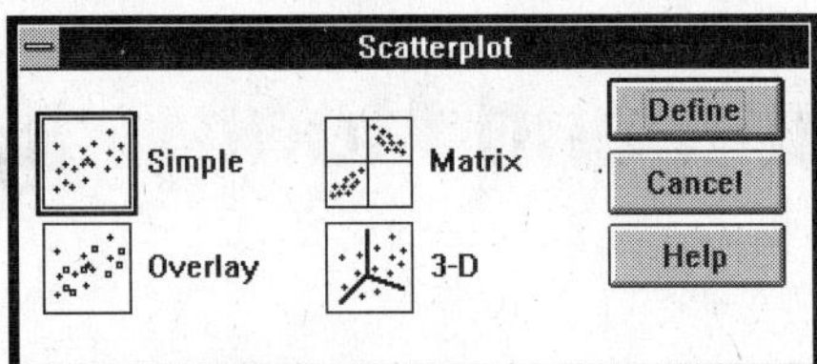

❷ Click on Define.

This opens the Simple Scatterplot dialog box, as shown in Figure 6.2.

Figure 6.2 Simple Scatterplot dialog box

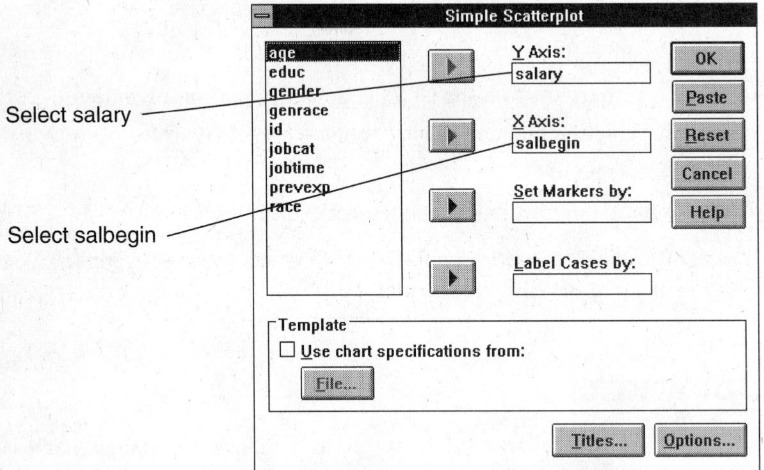

❸ Select *salary* for the Y Axis.

❹ Select *salbegin* for the X Axis.

❺ Click on OK.

The chart is displayed in the Chart Carousel, as shown in Figure 6.3.

Figure 6.3 Scatterplot in Chart Carousel

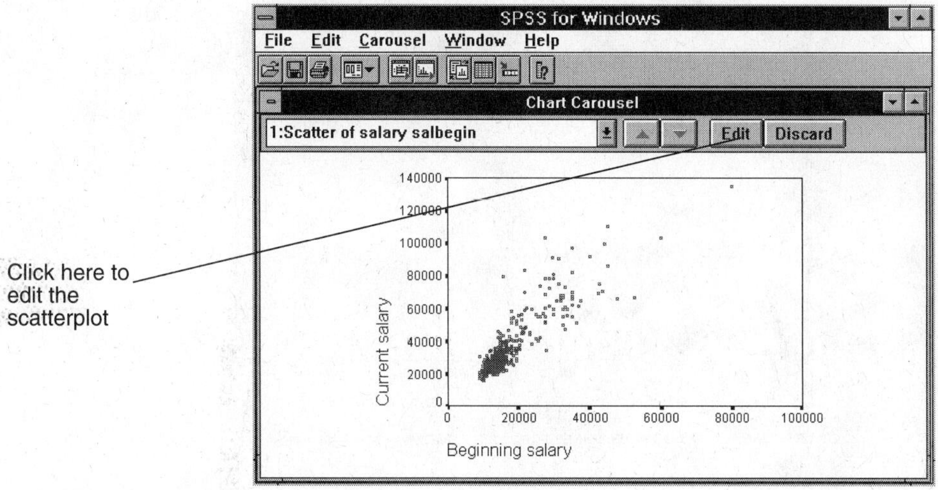

Click here to edit the scatterplot

Editing the Chart

You can open more than one chart window at once, and you must open a separate window for each chart you want to edit.

To modify the chart, you need to move it from the Chart Carousel into a chart window.

1. To place the scatterplot in a chart window, click on Edit on the Chart Carousel toolbar.

This opens a chart window containing the scatterplot, as shown in Figure 6.4, with the chart window menu bar and toolbar displayed.

Figure 6.4 Scatterplot in a chart window

Chart window menu bar and toolbar

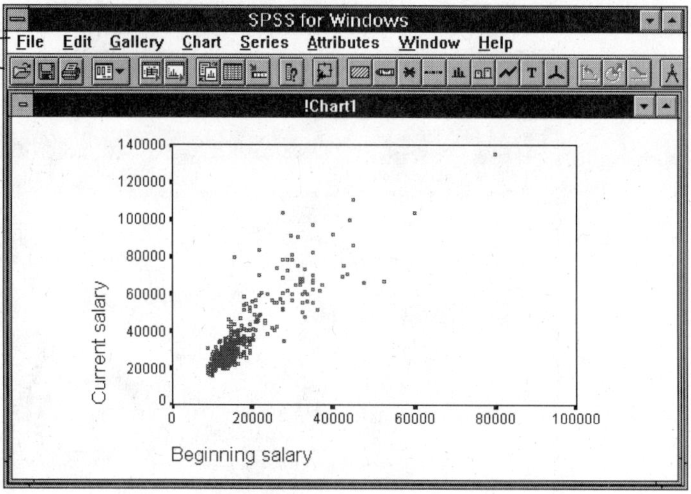

Using Point Selection Mode to Identify Points

Examining your scatterplot, you notice one person whose salary has increased from roughly $30,000 to more that $100,000 (as indicated in Figure 6.5). To find out more about this individual, you can use point selection mode.

Figure 6.5 Scatterplot in a chart window

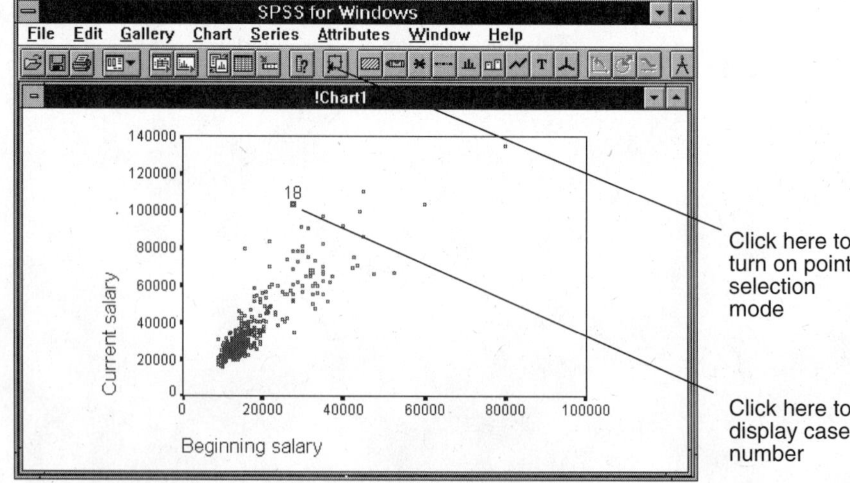

With a boxplot or scatterplot in the active chart window, click on

The cursor changes to

indicating that point selection is on.

Click here to turn on point selection mode

Click here to display case number

2. Click on [icon] on the toolbar.

   This turns on point selection mode.

3. Click on the point indicated in Figure 6.5.

   The value 18 is displayed, indicating that the case in question is case number 18.

4. Click on [icon] on the toolbar.

   This activates the Data Editor, with case number 18 selected, as shown in Figure 6.6.

Figure 6.6 Data Editor with case selected

c:\spsssv\employee.sav

18:id 18

	id	gender	race	genrace	age	educ	jobcat	salary	salbegin
16	16	Male	Whit	White m	30	12	Clerica	40800	15000
17	17	Male	Whit	White m	32	15	Clerica	46000	14250
18	18	Male	Whit	White m	37	16	Salarie	103750	27510
19	19	Male	Whit	White m	32	12	Clerica	42300	14250
20	20	Female	Whit	White fe	54	12	Clerica	26250	11550

5. After you are finished examining the data, click on [icon] to return to the scatterplot.

6. Click on point number 18 again to deselect it.

   The displayed value 18 disappears.

7. Click on [icon] again.

   This turns off point selection mode.

Adding a Regression Line

The scatterplot appears linear.

8. To draw a line that fits the distribution of points, from the menus choose:

   Chart
    Options...

   This opens the Scatterplot Options dialog box, as shown in Figure 6.7.

Figure 6.7 Scatterplot Options dialog box

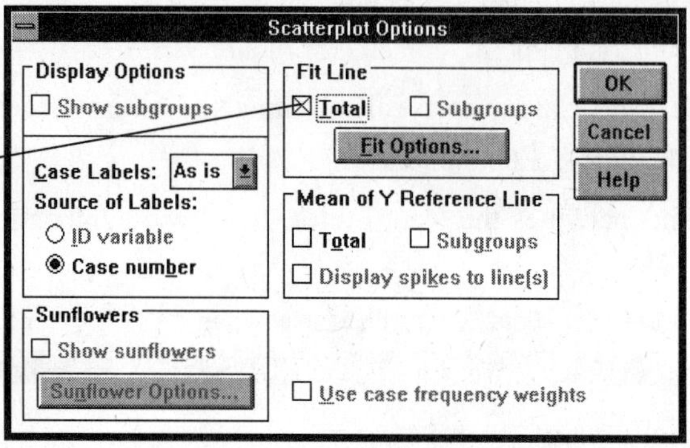

❾ In the Fit Line group, click on Total.

All of the points will be used when the position of the line is calculated.

❿ Click on OK.

This places a regression line on the scatterplot. (Figure 6.10 on p. 58 shows the finished scatterplot.)

Changing the Scale Axis

Suppose you want to see cases with beginning salaries below $40,000 in more detail. You can change the scale of the *x*-axis so that only these cases are displayed.

⓫ Double-click on one of the numbers in the horizontal axis (or choose Axis from the Chart menu, select X scale, and click on OK).

This opens the X Scale Axis dialog box, as shown in Figure 6.8.

Figure 6.8 X Scale Axis dialog box

Change Maximum to 40000

⓬ In the Range group box, change the maximum displayed from 100000 to 40000.

⓭ Click on OK.

Figure 6.10 on p. 58 shows the finished scatterplot.

Adding a Title

You can customize your chart by adding a title.

⓮ To add a title to the chart, from the menus choose:

Chart
  Title...

This opens the Titles dialog box, as shown in Figure 6.9.

Figure 6.9 Titles dialog box

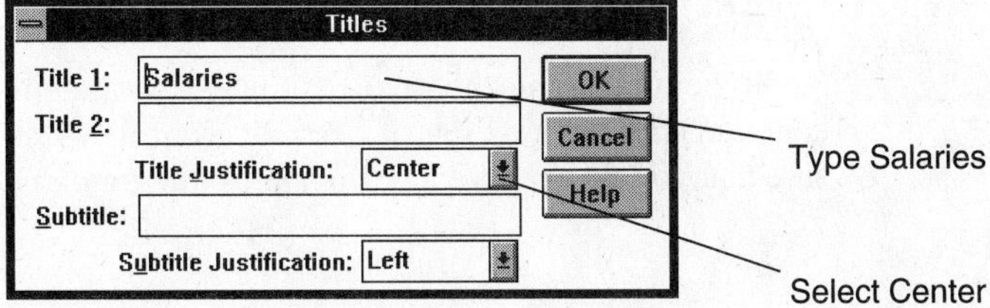

⓯ Type **Salaries** in the Title 1 text box.

16. To center the title, select Center from the Title Justification drop-down list.
17. Click on OK.

The title is displayed, as shown in Figure 6.10.

Figure 6.10 Scatterplot with regression line, title, and modified x-axis

Although cases with beginning salaries greater than $40,000 are not displayed, they are still used to calculate the regression line.

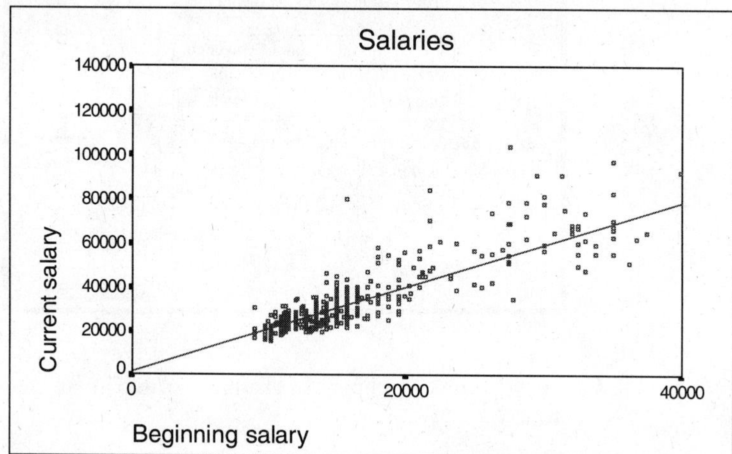

Saving the Chart

If you want to save the chart, you must do so before exiting from SPSS.

1. With the scatterplot in the active window, from the menus choose:

   File
   Save Chart

2. Enter a name for the chart and click on OK.

What's Next?

At this point, you can choose to continue experimenting with the Graphs menu, continue with the next tutorial, or exit from SPSS. If you exit from SPSS, be sure that you *do not* save any changes to the *employee.sav* data file.

7 Tutorial: Modifying Data Values

SPSS provides numerous facilities for modifying data values and creating new variables based on transformations of existing variables. This tutorial introduces the use of the SPSS Transform menu and demonstrates the use of the Recode option to recode a continuous variable into distinct categories.

This tutorial uses the data file *employee.sav*, described in previous chapters. If you need help in opening the file in SPSS, see Chapter 4.

Recoding Data Values

One of the most useful data transformations is accomplished with the Recode facility, which is used to combine categories of a variable.

For example, if you want to show the relationship between salary and gender in a simple crosstabulation, you can't use actual salaries in a crosstabulation because very few people are likely to have the same salary. The number of distinct "categories" for salary would likely be almost as large as the number of cases in your data file. You could, however, create a new variable that combines salary ranges into a small number of categories, such as less than $25,000, $25,000 to $49,999, and $50,000 or more.

❶ From the menus choose:

Transform
  Recode ▸
    Into Different Variables...

This opens the Recode into Different Variables dialog box.

❷ Select *salary* on the variable list and click on ▸ to move it to the Numeric Variable -> Output Variable list, as shown in Figure 7.1.

To recode a string variable into consecutive integer values, you can use the Automatic Recode option on the Transform menu.

Figure 7.1 Recode into Different Variables dialog box

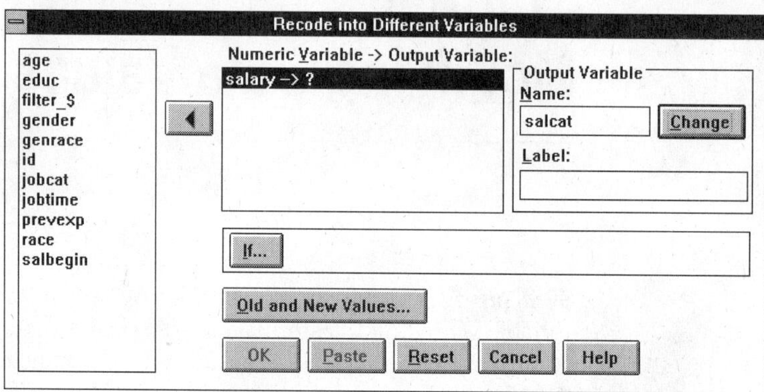

3. In the Output Variable group, type **salcat** in the Name text box.
4. Click on Change.

   The original variable name and the new variable name are displayed together on the Numeric Variable -> Output Variable list.

5. Click on Old and New Values....

   This opens the Old and New Values dialog box, as shown in Figure 7.2.

Figure 7.2 Old and New Values dialog box

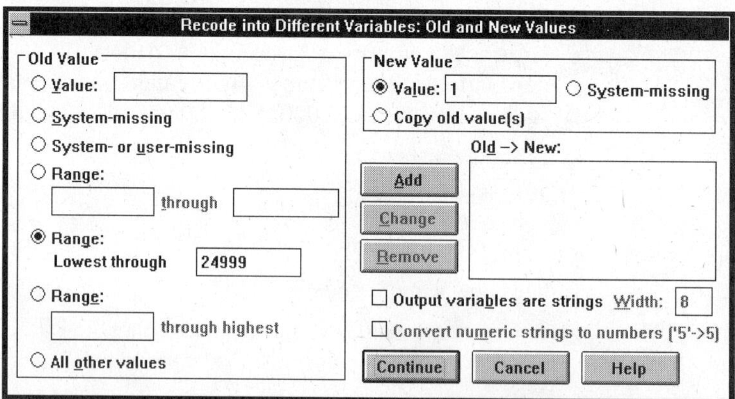

6. In the Old Value group, select Range: Lowest through.
7. Type **24999** in the Lowest through text box.
8. In the New Value group, select Value.

9. Type **1** in the Value text box.
10. Click on Add.

    Lowest thru 24999 -> 1 is displayed on the Old -> New list (see Figure 7.3). This means that all salaries below $25,000 will be combined into a single category coded 1 for the new variable *salcat*.

11. In the Old Value group, select Range.
12. Type **25000** in the first Range text box.
13. Type **49999** in the second Range text box.
14. In the New Value group, select Value, type **2** in the text box, and then click on Add.
15. In the Old Value group, select Range: through highest and type **50000** in the text box.
16. In the New Value group, select Value, type **3** in the text box, and then click on Add.

    The Old and New Values dialog box should now look like Figure 7.3.

Figure 7.3 Completed Old and New Values dialog box

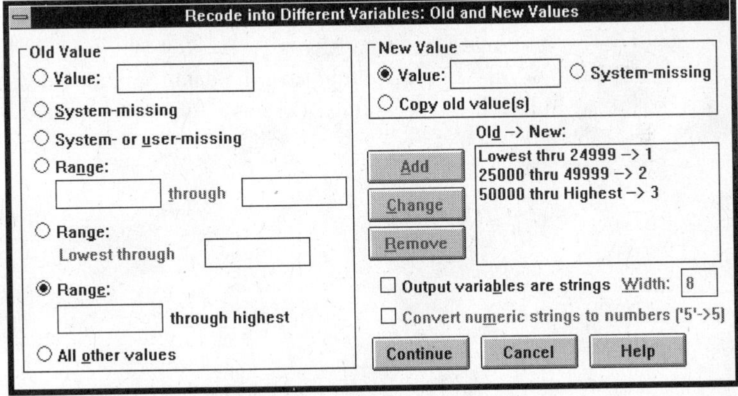

Any unspecified old values will be set to system-missing for the new variable. If you don't want to recode all values, select All other values and select Copy old value(s) to retain values not covered by the recoding scheme.

If SPSS does not calculate values for the new variable after you click on OK, select Run Pending Transformations from the Transform menu.

⑰ Click on Continue in the Old and New Values dialog box, and then click on OK in the main Recode into Different Variables dialog box.

The new variable *salcat* is added to the data file and is displayed after *prevexp* in the Data Editor window. You can add descriptive value labels for the numeric category codes by using the Define Variable option on the Data menu (see Chapter 3 for more information on defining variables).

Note: If SPSS does not calculate values for the new variable after you click on OK, select Run Pending Transformations from the Transform menu. (If you want SPSS to always run your transformations immediately, select Preferences from the Edit menu. In the Preferences dialog box, be sure that the option Calculate values immediately is selected in the Transformation and Merge Options group.)

What's Next?

At this point, you can exit from SPSS or continue with the next tutorial. If you exit from SPSS and you have changed the data file in any way, you will be asked whether you want to save the changes. *Do not* save changes to the *employee.sav* data file.

Note: If you want to save the data file with the new variable created in this tutorial, you should use the Save As option on the File menu and give the file a new name.

8 Tutorial: Working with Syntax

This tutorial introduces the use of command syntax, an alternate way to run procedures. Using syntax also allows you to save the exact specifications used during an SPSS session. This tutorial demonstrates the following:

- Pasting syntax from a dialog box
- Typing syntax into a syntax window
- Editing syntax

This tutorial uses the data file *employee.sav*, described in previous chapters. If you need help in opening the file in SPSS, see Chapter 4.

Pasting Syntax

The easiest way to construct a useful command is to paste the syntax from a dialog box. In this example, command syntax will be used to run the Frequencies procedure. The results are similar to those shown in Chapter 1.

❶ From the menus choose:

Statistics
  Summarize
    Frequencies...

This opens the Frequencies dialog box.

❷ Select *jobcat* and move it to the Variable(s) list.

❸ Click on Charts.

❹ In the Charts dialog box, select Bar chart(s), and in the Axis Label Display group, select Percentages. Then click on Continue.

The Frequencies dialog box is displayed, as shown in Figure 8.1.

Figure 8.1 Frequencies dialog box

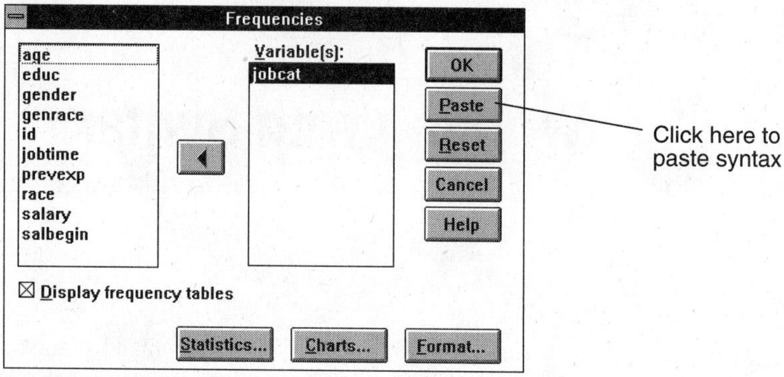

❺ Click on Paste (instead of OK).

This opens a syntax window and pastes the FREQUENCIES command into it, as shown in Figure 8.2.

Figure 8.2 Syntax window

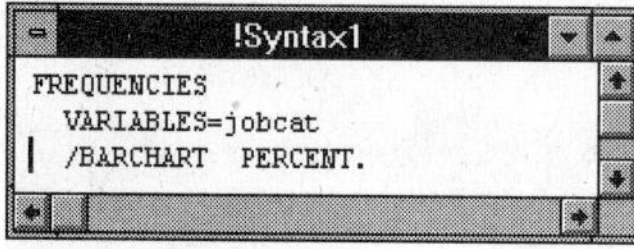

To run several commands, highlight the commands and click on .

❻ To run the command, make sure the cursor is within the command, and click on the Run Syntax tool .

The results are the same as if you had clicked on OK in the Frequencies dialog box.

Editing Syntax

In the syntax window, you can edit the syntax. For example, you could change the subcommand /BARCHART to display frequencies instead of percentages, as shown in Figure 8.3. (A subcommand is indicated by a slash.)

Figure 8.3 Modified syntax

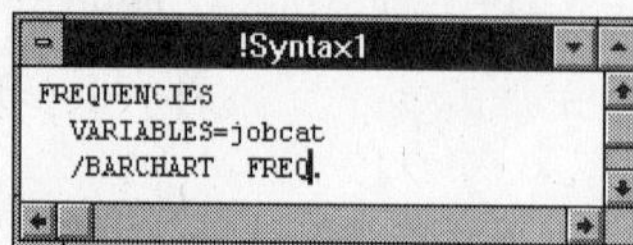

To find out what subcommands and keywords are available for the current command, click on the Syntax Help tool . Complete syntax for the FREQUENCIES command is shown in Figure 8.4.

Figure 8.4 FREQUENCIES syntax

```
Help: SPSS for Windows
File  Edit  Bookmark  Help
Contents  Search  Back  History  <<  >>
Frequencies Syntax

FREQUENCIES [VARIABLES=]varlist[(min,max)]
                        [varlist...]
 [/FORMAT=[{CONDENSE}][{NOTABLE }]
           {ONEPAGE }  {LIMIT(n)}
          [NOLABELS] [WRITE]
          [{DVALUE}][DOUBLE][NEWPAGE][INDEX]]
           {AFREQ }
           {DFREQ }
 [/MISSING=INCLUDE]
 [/BARCHART=[MIN(n)][MAX(n)][{FREQ(n)    }]]
                             {PERCENT(n)}
 [/HISTOGRAM=[MIN(n)][MAX(n)][{FREQ(n)    }]
                              {PERCENT(n)}
             [{NONORMAL}][INCREMENT(n)]]
              {NORMAL  }
 [/HBAR=[MIN(n)][MAX(n)][{FREQ(n)    }]
                         {PERCENT(n)}
        [{NONORMAL}][INCREMENT(n)]]
         {NORMAL  }
 [/NTILES=n]
 [/PERCENTILES=value list]
 [/STATISTICS=[DEFAULT][MEAN][STDDEV][SUM]
              [MINIMUM][MAXIMUM][RANGE]
              [SEMEAN][VARIANCE][SKEWNESS][SESKEW]
              [MODE][KURTOSIS][SEKURT][MEDIAN]
              [ALL][NONE]]
 [/GROUPED=varlist [{(width)         }]]
                    {(boundary list)}

Click here for other commands.
```

If the cursor is not in a command, clicking on the Syntax Help tool displays an alphabetical list of commands. You can click on the one you want.

Typing Syntax

You can type syntax into a syntax window that is already open, or you can open a new syntax window by choosing:

File
  New
    SPSS Syntax

Saving Syntax

To save a syntax file, from the menus choose:

File
  Save SPSS Syntax

or

File
  Save As...

This opens a standard Windows dialog box for saving files.

Opening and Running a Syntax File

To open a saved syntax file, from the menus choose:

File
  Open
    SPSS Syntax...

Then run the commands by using the Run Syntax tool, as described above. If the commands apply to a specific data file, the data file must be opened before running the commands, or you must include a command that opens the data file. You can paste this type of command from the dialog boxes that open data files.

Additional Information

In the Help system, most procedures have a topic that discusses additional features available with command language. For more information about how to use syntax, you can search the Help system for Syntax. You can also consult the *SPSS Base System Syntax Reference Guide* that comes with SPSS for Windows.

What's Next?

At this point, you can exit from SPSS. When you exit from SPSS and you have changed the data file in any way, you will be asked whether you want to save the changes. *Do not* save changes to the *employee.sav* data file.

The next chapter describes data files in different formats.

9 Data Files

Data files come in a wide variety of formats, and SPSS is designed to handle many of them, including:

- Spreadsheet files created with Lotus 1-2-3, Excel, and Multiplan
- Database files created with dBASE
- Tab-delimited and other types of ASCII text files
- SPSS data files created on other operating systems

Creating a New Data File

If your data are not already in computer files, you can use the Data Editor to enter the data and create an SPSS data file. The Data Editor is a simple, efficient spreadsheet-like facility that opens automatically when you start an SPSS session. For information on the Data Editor, see Chapter 3.

Opening a Data File

To open an SPSS, spreadsheet, dBASE, or tab-delimited data file, from the menus choose:

File
  Open ▸
    Data...

This opens the Open Data File dialog box, as shown in Figure 9.1.

Select the file type from the drop-down list. If the extension of your data file is different from the default extension for the file type, enter a wildcard search with the extension in the File Name text box.

Figure 9.1 Open Data File dialog box

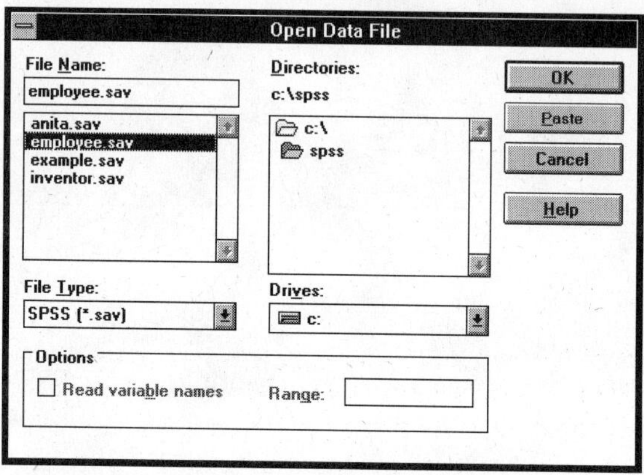

Specifying File Type

Before you can open a data file, you need to tell SPSS what type of file it is. SPSS needs to know the file type regardless of the file extension. To change the file type, you must change the selection on the drop-down list. You cannot specify a different file type simply by changing the extension of the wildcard search in the File Name text box.

Reading Variable Names

For Lotus, Excel, SYLK, and tab-delimited files, you can read variable names from the file. The values in the first row of the file (or cell range) are used as variable names. If variable names exceed eight characters, they are truncated. If they are not unique, SPSS modifies them.

Reading a Range of Cells

For Lotus, Excel, and SYLK files, you can specify a range of cells to read.

- For Lotus files, specify the beginning column letter and row number, two periods, and the ending column letter and row number (for example, A1..K14).
- For Excel files, specify the beginning column letter and row number, a colon, and the ending column letter and row number (for example, A1:K14).

- For SYLK files and Excel files saved in R1C1 display format, specify the beginning and ending cells of the range separated by a colon (for example, R1C1:R14C11).

If you have defined a name for a range of cells in the spreadsheet file, you can enter the name in the Range text box.

How SPSS Reads Spreadsheet Data

An SPSS data file is rectangular. The boundaries (or dimensions) of the data file are determined by the number of cases (rows) and variables (columns). There are no "empty" cells within the boundaries of the data file. All cells have a value, even if that value is "blank." The following general rules apply to reading spreadsheet data:

If your spreadsheet is organized with cases in columns and variables in rows, use the Transpose option on the Data menu to put your data in the correct order after you read the data into SPSS.

- Rows are considered cases, and columns are considered variables.
- The number of variables is determined by the last column with any nonblank cells or the total number of nonblank cells in the row containing variable names. If you read variable names, any columns with a blank cell for the variable name are not included in the data file.
- The number of cases is determined by the last row with any nonblank cells within the column boundaries defined by the number of variables (unless you read a range of cells).
- The data type and width for each variable are determined by the column width and data type of the first data cell in the column. Values of other types are converted to the system-missing value. If the first data cell in the column is blank, the global default data type for the spreadsheet (usually numeric) is used.
- For numeric variables, blank cells are converted to the system-missing value, indicated by a period.
- For string variables, a blank is a valid string value, and blank cells are treated as valid string values.
- If you don't read variable names from the spreadsheet, SPSS uses the column letters (A, B, C, etc.) for variable names for Excel and Lotus files. For SYLK files and Excel files saved in R1C1 display format, SPSS uses the column number preceded by the letter C for variable names (*C1*, *C2*, *C3*, etc.).

Figure 9.2 shows how SPSS reads a spreadsheet file that contains variable names, and Figure 9.3 shows how SPSS reads an Excel spreadsheet file that has no variable names.

Figure 9.2 Reading spreadsheet data with variable names

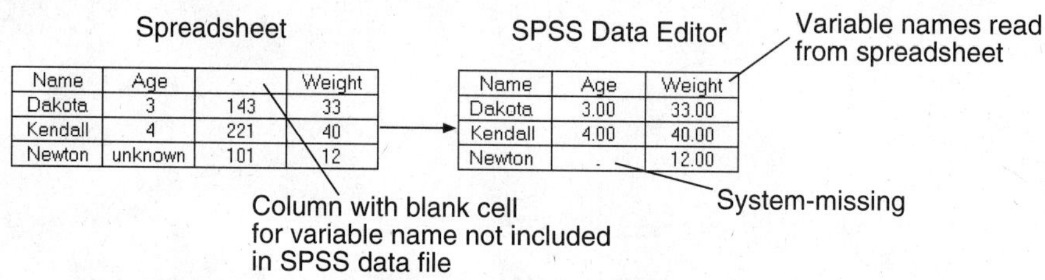

Figure 9.3 Reading Excel spreadsheet file without variable names

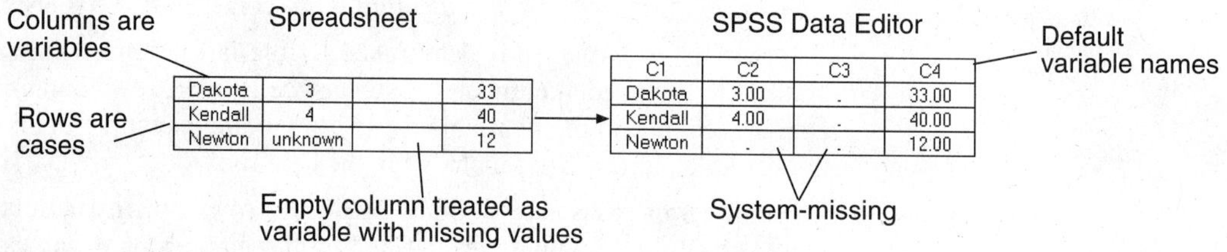

How SPSS Reads dBASE Files

Database files are logically very similar to SPSS data files. The following general rules apply to dBASE files:

- Field names are automatically translated to SPSS variable names.
- Field names should comply with SPSS variable-naming conventions (see “Defining Fixed Variables” on p. 72). Field names longer than eight characters are truncated. If the first eight characters of the field name don’t produce a unique name, the field is dropped.
- Colons used in dBASE field names are translated to underscores.
- Records marked for deletion but not actually purged are included. SPSS creates a new string variable, *D_R*, which contains an asterisk for cases marked for deletion.

How SPSS Reads Tab-Delimited Files

The following general rules apply to reading tab-delimited files:

- Values can be either numeric or string. Any value that contains non-numeric characters is considered a string value. (Formats such as Dollar and Date are not recognized and are read as string values.)
- The data type and width for each variable are determined by the type and width of the first data value in the column. Values of other types are converted to the system-missing value.
- For numeric variables, the assigned width is eight digits or the number of digits in the first data value, whichever is greater. Values that exceed the defined width are rounded for display. The entire value is stored internally.
- For string variables, values that exceed the defined width are truncated.
- If you don't read variable names from the file, SPSS assigns the default names *var1*, *var2*, *var3*, etc.

Reading Text Files

If your raw data are in simple text files (standard ASCII format), you can read the data in SPSS and assign variable names and data formats. To read a text file, from the menus choose:

File
  Read ASCII Data...

This opens the Read ASCII Data File dialog box, as shown in Figure 9.4.

Figure 9.4 Read ASCII Data File dialog box

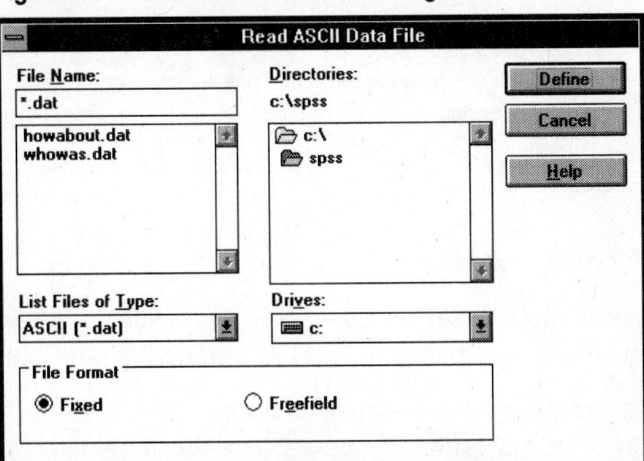

File Format

There are two alternatives for file format:

- **Fixed.** Each variable is recorded in the same column location on the same record (line) for each case in the data file. This is the default.
- **Freefield.** The variables are recorded in the same order for each case, but not necessarily in the same locations. Spaces are interpreted as delimiters between values. More than one case can be recorded on a single line. After reading the value for the last defined variable for a case, SPSS reads the next value encountered as the first variable for the next case.

Defining Fixed Variables

To define fixed-format data, select Fixed for the File Format in the Read ASCII Data File dialog box and click on Define. This opens the Define Fixed Variables dialog box, as shown in Figure 9.5.

Figure 9.5 Define Fixed Variables dialog box

Define Fixed Variables
File: C:\SPSSWIN\HOWABOUT.DAT
Defined Variables:
Name:
Record: 1
Start Column:
End Column:
Data Type
123=123, 1.23=1.23
Numeric as is
Add Change Remove
OK Paste Reset Cancel Help
Value Assigned to Blanks for Numeric Variables
System missing
Value:
Display summary table
Display warning message for undefined data

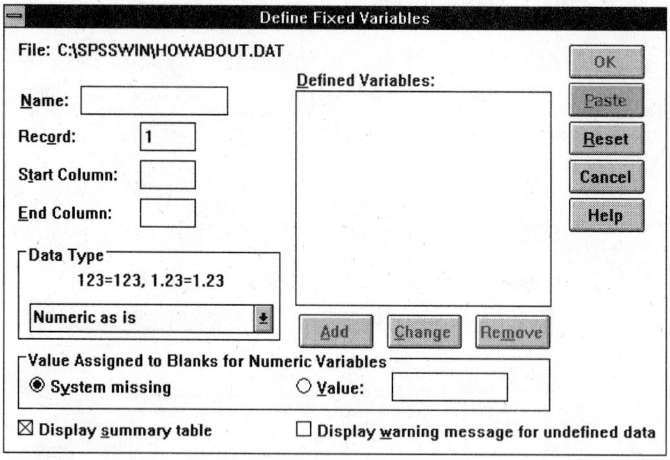

For each variable, you must specify the following:

Name. Variable names must begin with a letter and cannot exceed eight characters. Each variable name must be unique. Variable names are not case sensitive.

Record. A case can have data on more than one line. The **record number** indicates the line within the case where the variable is located.

Start Column/End Column. These two column specifications indicate the location of the variable within the record. The value for a variable can appear anywhere within the range of columns. With the exception of string variables, leading blank spaces in the column range are ignored.

Data Type. Select a data type from the drop-down list. When you select a data type, an example is displayed above the drop-down list.

Entering Variable Definitions

To enter a variable definition:

1. Specify the variable name, record and column locations, and data type.
2. Click on Add. The record number, start and end columns, variable name, and data type appear on the Defined Variables list, as shown in Figure 9.6.

Figure 9.6 Defined Variables

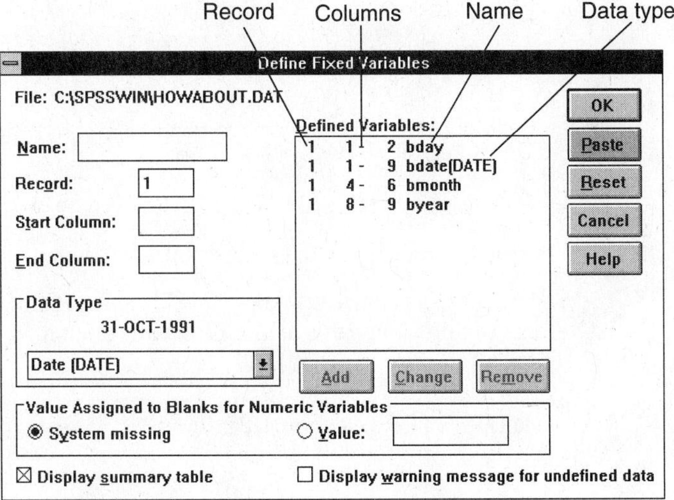

The following general rules apply:

- You can enter variables in any order. They are automatically sorted by record and start column.
- You can specify multiple variables in the same or overlapping column locations. For example, in Figure 9.6, *bday* is in columns 1–2, *bmonth* in columns 4–6, *byear* in columns 8–9, and *bdate* in columns 1–9.
- You can read selective data fields and/or records. You don't have to define or read all the data in the file. SPSS reads only the columns and records you specify and skips over any data you don't define.

Defining Freefield Variables

To define freefield format data, select Freefield for the File Format in the Read ASCII Data File dialog box and click on Define. This opens the Define Freefield Variables dialog box, as shown in Figure 9.7.

Figure 9.7 Define Freefield Variables dialog box

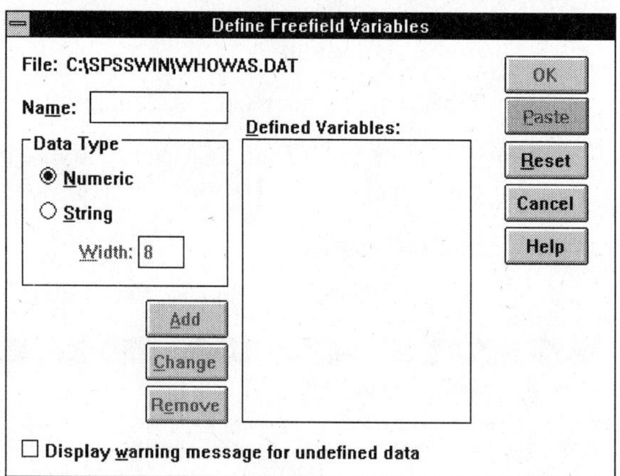

For each variable, you must specify the following:

Name. Variable names must begin with a letter and cannot exceed eight characters. Additional variable naming rules are given in "Defining Fixed Variables" on p. 72.

Data Type. For freefield format, data can be either numeric or string (alphanumeric).

Entering Variable Definitions

To enter a variable definition, specify the variable name and data type and click on Add. The variable appears on the Defined Variables list. If it is a string variable, the letter A and the defined width appear in parentheses next to the variable name.

While defining data in freefield format is relatively simple and easy, it is also easy to make mistakes. Keep the following rules in mind:

- You must enter variables in the order in which they appear in the data file. Each new variable definition is added to the bottom of the list, and SPSS reads the variables in that order.

- You must provide definitions for all variables in the file. If you omit any, the data file will be read incorrectly. SPSS determines the end of one case and the beginning of the next based on the number of defined variables.
- The data file cannot contain any missing data. Blank fields are read as delimiters between variables, and SPSS does not distinguish between single and multiple blanks. If a single observation is missing, the entire remainder of the data file will be read incorrectly.
- If your Windows International settings (accessed from the Control Panel) use a period as the decimal indicator, SPSS interprets commas as delimiters that separate data values in freefield format. For example, a value of 1,234 is read as two separate values: 1 and 234.

Saving a Data File

You can save data files in any of the following formats:

- SPSS
- SPSS/PC+
- SPSS portable format (for use on other operating systems)
- Lotus 1-2-3
- Excel
- SYLK (symbolic link)
- dBASE
- Tab-delimited ASCII text
- Fixed-format ASCII text

To save a new SPSS data file or to save the data in a different file format:

1. Make the Data Editor the active window (by clicking anywhere in the Data Editor).
2. From the menus choose:

   File
     Save As...

This opens the Save Data As dialog box, as shown in Figure 9.8.

Figure 9.8 Save Data As dialog box

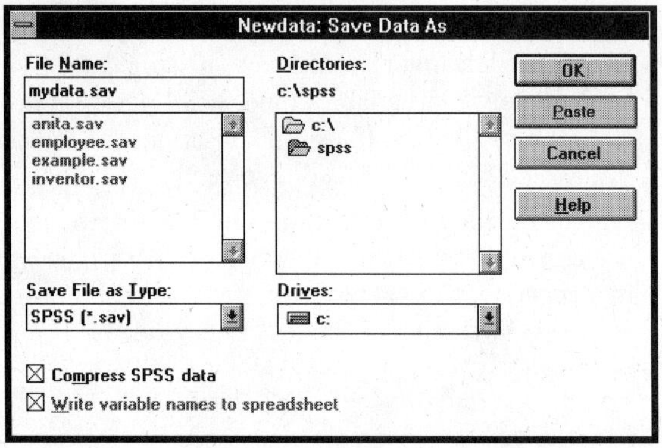

Specifying File Type

Before you can save a data file, you need to tell SPSS what type of file it is. SPSS needs to know the file type regardless of the file extension. To change the file type, you must change the selection on the drop-down list. You cannot specify a different file type simply by changing the extension of the wildcard search in the File Name text box.

Closing a Data File

Since only one data file can be open at a time, SPSS automatically closes the working data file before it opens another one. If there have been any changes to the data file since it was last saved, SPSS asks if you want to save the changes before it closes the file and opens the next one.

10 Calculating New Data Values

In an ideal situation, your raw data are perfectly suitable for the type of analysis you want to perform. Unfortunately, this is rarely the case. Preliminary analysis may reveal inconvenient coding schemes or coding errors, or data transformations may be required in order to coax out the true relationship between variables.

With SPSS, you can perform data transformations ranging from simple tasks, such as collapsing categories for analysis, to creating new variables based on complex equations and conditional statements.

Recoding Values

You can modify data values by recoding them. This is particularly useful for combining categories. You can recode the values within existing variables, or you can create new variables based on the recoded values of existing variables. For more information on recoding, see Chapter 7.

Computing Values

To compute values for a variable based on numeric transformations of other variables, from the menus choose:

Transform
  Compute...

This opens the Compute Variable dialog box, as shown in Figure 10.1.

Figure 10.1 Compute Variable dialog box

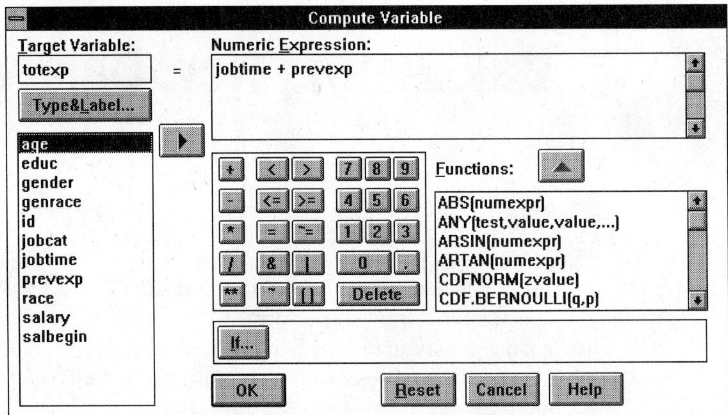

To compute a variable:

1. Enter a target variable name. If you enter an existing variable name, the computed values replace the original values.
2. Enter the numeric expression for the computed value. If the computed value is based on the values of existing variables, you can select the variable names from the variable list.

For example, in Figure 10.1, the new variable *totexp* will be computed as the sum of variables *jobtime* and *prevexp*.

Calculator Pad

The calculator pad contains numbers, arithmetic operators, relational operators, and logical operators (see Table 10.1). You can use it like a calculator (using the mouse to point and click on keys) or simply as a reference for the correct symbols to use for various operators.

Table 10.1 Calculator pad operators

Arithmetic Operators		Relational Operators		Logical Operators	
+	Addition	<	Less than	&	And. Both relations must be true.
–	Subtraction	>	Greater than	|	Or. Either relation can be true.
*	Multiplication	<=	Less than or equal to	~	Not. Reverses the true/false outcome of the expression.
/	Division	>=	Greater than or equal to		
**	Exponentiation	=	Equal to		
( )	Order of operations	~=	Not equal to		

Arithmetic Operators

Since fairly complex expressions are possible, it is important to keep in mind the order in which operations are performed. Functions are evaluated first, followed by exponentiation, then multiplication and division, and finally addition and subtraction. You can control the order of operations by enclosing in parentheses the operation you want to be executed first. You can use the ( ) key on the calculator pad to enclose a highlighted portion of the expression in parentheses.

Relational Operators

A **relation** is a logical expression that compares two values using a relational operator. They are primarily used in conditional transformations (see "Relational and Logical Operators in Conditional Expressions" on p. 81).

Logical Operators

You can use logical operators to join two relations or reverse the true/false outcome of a conditional expression. They are primarily used in conditional transformations (see "Relational and Logical Operators in Conditional Expressions" on p. 81).

Functions

The function list contains over 70 built-in functions, including:

- Arithmetic functions
- Statistical functions
- Distribution functions
- Logical functions
- Date and time aggregation and extraction functions
- Missing-value functions

- Cross-case functions
- String functions

For information on specific functions, click on Help in the Compute Variable dialog box.

Pasting and Editing Functions

Pasting a Function into an Expression. To paste a function into an expression:

1. Position the cursor in the expression at the point where you want the function to appear.
2. Double-click on the function on the Functions list (or select the function and click on the [▲] pushbutton).

The function is inserted into the expression. If you highlight part of the expression and then insert the function, the highlighted portion of the expression is used as the first argument in the function.

Editing a Function in an Expression. The function isn't complete until you enter the arguments, represented by question marks in the pasted function. The number of question marks indicates the minimum number of arguments required to complete the function. To edit a function:

1. Highlight the question mark(s) in the pasted function.
2. Enter the arguments. If the arguments are variable names, you can paste them from the variable list.

Conditional Expressions

You can use conditional expressions (also called logical expressions) to apply transformations to selected subsets of cases. A **conditional expression** returns a value of true, false, or missing for each case. If the result of a conditional expression is true, the transformation is applied to that case. If the result is false or missing, the transformation is not applied to the case.

To specify a conditional expression, click on If... in the Compute Variable dialog box. This opens the Compute Variable If Cases dialog box, as shown in Figure 10.2.

Figure 10.2 Compute Variable If Cases dialog box

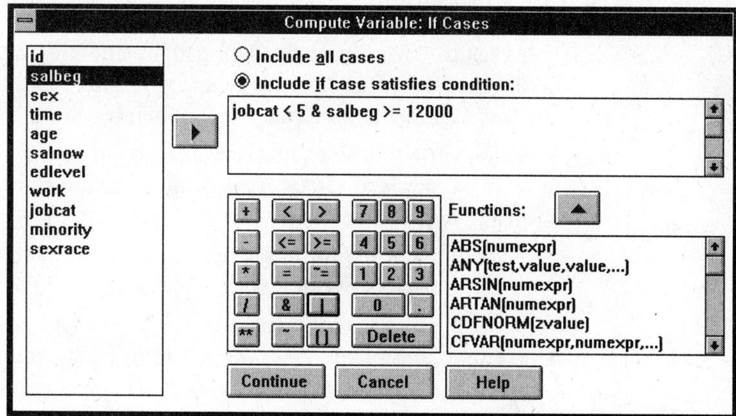

To specify a conditional expression:

1. Select Include if case satisfies condition.
2. Enter the conditional expression.

Relational and Logical Operators in Conditional Expressions

Most conditional expressions contain at least one relational operator, as in

age>=21

or

salary*3<100000

In the first example, only cases with a value of 21 or greater for *age* are selected. In the second example, *salary* multiplied by 3 must be less than 100,000 for a case to be selected.

You can also link two or more conditional expressions using logical operators, as in

age>=21 | jobcat=1

or

salary*3<100000 & jobcat~=5

In the first example, cases that meet either the *age* condition or the *jobcat* condition are selected. In the second example, both the *salary* and *jobcat* conditions must be met for a case to be selected.

Rules for Expressions

Items selected from the calculator pad, function list, and variable list are pasted in the correct format. If you type an expression in the text box or edit part of it (such as arguments for a function), remember the following simple rules:

- String variable values must be enclosed in apostrophes or quotation marks, as in **NAME='Fred'**. If the string value includes an apostrophe, enclose the string in quotation marks.
- The argument list for a function must be enclosed in parentheses. You can insert a space between the argument name and the parentheses, but none is required.
- Multiple arguments in a function must be separated by commas. You can insert spaces between arguments, but none is required.
- Each relation in a complex expression must be complete by itself. For example, **age>=18 & age<35** is correct, while **age>=18 & <35** generates an error.
- A period (.) is the only valid decimal indicator in expressions, regardless of your Windows International settings.

Additional Data Transformations

The following additional data transformations are also available on the Transform menu:

- **Count Occurrences**. Counts occurrences of the same value(s) across a list of variables within each case.
- **Rank Cases**. Computes ranks and normal and Savage scores, and classifies cases into groups based on percentile values.
- **Automatic Recode**. Recodes string and numeric variables into consecutive integers. This is useful for SPSS procedures that require integer data.
- **Create Time Series**. Creates new time series variables based on functions of existing time series variables. (Any variable measured regularly over a period of time is a time series variable.)
- **Replace Missing Values**. Replaces missing values in time series data with estimates computed with one of several methods.

11 Sorting and Selecting Data

Data files are not always organized in the ideal form for your specific needs. SPSS offers a wide range of file transformation capabilities, including the ability to:

- **Sort data**. You can sort cases based on the value of one or more variables.
- **Select subsets of cases**. You can restrict your analysis to a subset of cases or perform simultaneous analyses on different subsets.

Sorting Data

Sorting cases (sorting rows of the data file) is often useful—and sometimes necessary—for certain types of analysis. To reorder the sequence of cases in the data file based on the value of one or more sorting variables, from the menus choose:

Data
 Sort Cases...

This opens the Sort Cases dialog box, as shown in Figure 11.1.

Figure 11.1 Sort Cases dialog box

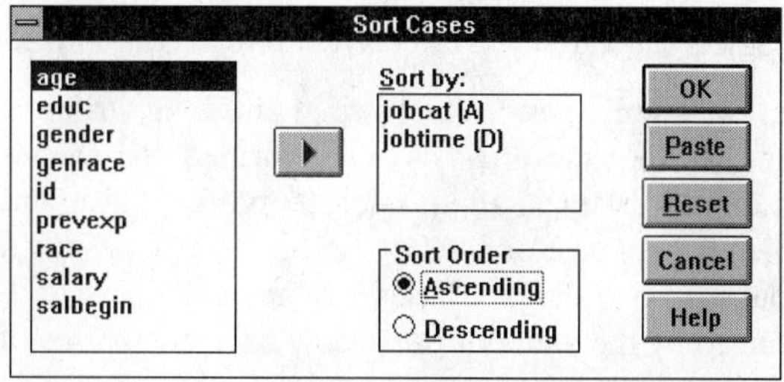

If you select multiple sort variables, the order in which they appear on the Sort list determines the order in which cases are sorted. For example, based on the Sort list in Figure 11.1, cases will be sorted by descending value of *jobtime*

within ascending categories of *jobcat.* For string variables, uppercase letters precede their lowercase counterparts in sort order (for example, the string value "Yes" comes before "yes" in sort order).

Split-File Processing

To split your data file into separate groups for analysis, from the menus choose:

Data
 Split File...

This opens the Split File dialog box, as shown in Figure 11.2.

Figure 11.2 Split File dialog box

The Split FIle procedure automatically sorts the data file based on the values of the grouping variables. If the original order of cases is important, do not save the file after using Split File.

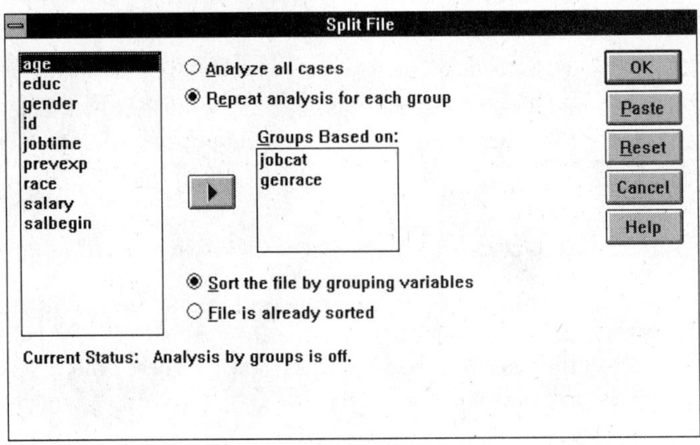

To split the data file into separate groups for analysis:

1. Select Repeat analysis for each group.
2. Select the variable(s) to use to split the file into separate groups.

You can use numeric, short string, and long string variables as grouping variables. A separate analysis is performed for each subgroup defined by the grouping variables. If you select multiple grouping variables, the order in which they appear on the Groups list determines the manner in which cases are grouped. For example, based on the Groups list in Figure 11.2, cases will be grouped by the value of *genrace* within categories of *jobcat.*

Sorting Cases for Split-File Processing

The Split File procedure creates a new subgroup each time it encounters a different value for one of the grouping variables. Therefore, it is important to sort cases based on the values of the grouping variables before invoking split-file processing.

By default, Split File automatically sorts the data file based on the values of the grouping variables. If the file is already sorted in the proper order, you can save processing time if you select File is already sorted.

Turning Split-File Processing On and Off

You can easily reopen the Split File dialog box by clicking on .

Once you invoke split-file processing, it remains in effect for the rest of the session unless you turn it off.

❍ **Analyze all cases.** Turns split-file processing off.

❍ **Repeat analysis for each group.** Turns split-file processing on.

If split-file processing is in effect, the message Split File on appears on the status bar at the bottom of the SPSS application window.

Selecting Subsets of Cases

You can restrict your analysis to a specific subgroup based on criteria that include variables and complex expressions. You can also select a random sample of cases. The criteria used to define a subgroup can include:

- Variable values and ranges
- Date and time ranges
- Case (row) numbers
- Arithmetic expressions
- Logical expressions
- Functions

To select a subset of cases for analysis, from the menus choose:

Data
 Select Cases...

This opens the Select Cases dialog box, as shown in Figure 11.3.

Figure 11.3 Select Cases dialog box

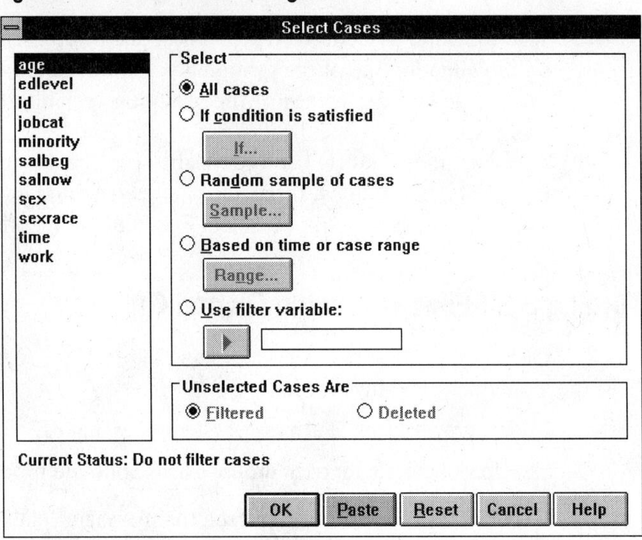

Unselected Cases

If you delete unselected cases and save the file, the cases cannot be recovered.

You can choose one of the following alternatives for the treatment of unselected cases:

❍ **Filtered**. Unselected cases are not included in the analysis but remain in the data file. You can use the unselected cases later in the session if you turn filtering off. If you select a random sample or if you select cases based on a conditional expression, this generates a variable named *filter_$* with a value of 1 for selected cases and a value of 0 for unselected cases.

❍ **Deleted**. Unselected cases are deleted from the data file. By reducing the number of cases in the open data file, you can save processing time. Deleted cases can be recovered only by exiting from the file without saving any changes and then reopening the file. The deletion of cases is permanent if you save the changes to the data file.

Selecting Cases Based on Conditional Expressions

To select cases based on a conditional expression, select If condition is satisfied and click on If... in the Select Cases dialog box. This opens the Select Cases If dialog box, as shown in Figure 11.4.

Figure 11.4 Select Cases If dialog box

The conditional expression can use existing variable names, constants, arithmetic operators, logical operators, relational operators, and functions. You can type and edit the expression in the text box just like text in a output window (see Chapter 4). You can also use the calculator pad, variable list, and function list to paste elements into the expression. See Chapter 10 for more information on working with conditional expressions.

Selecting a Random Sample

To obtain a random sample, select Random sample of cases in the Select Cases dialog box and click on Sample.... This opens the Select Cases Random Sample dialog box, as shown in Figure 11.5.

Figure 11.5 Select Cases Random Sample dialog box

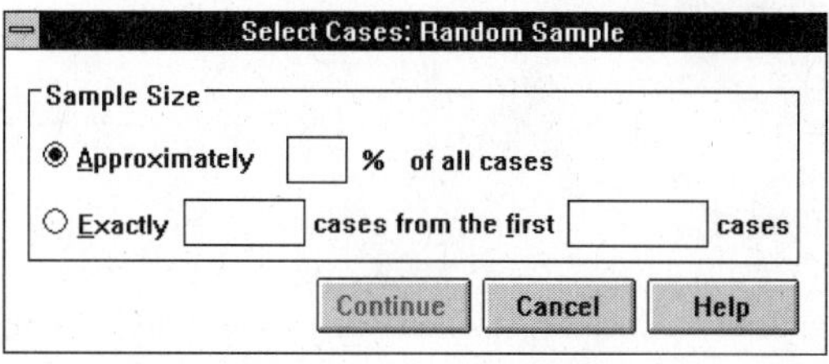

Sample Size. You can select one of the following alternatives for sample size:

❍ **Approximately**. A user-specified percentage. SPSS generates a random sample of approximately the specified percentage of cases.

❍ **Exactly**. A user-specified number of cases. You must also specify the number of cases from which to generate the sample. This second number should be less than or equal to the total number of cases in the data file. If the number exceeds the total number of cases in the data file, the sample will contain proportionally fewer cases than the requested number.

Selecting a Time Range or Case Range

To select a range of cases based on dates, times, or observation (row) number, select Based on time or case range and click on Range... in the Select Cases dialog box. This opens the Select Cases Range dialog box, as shown on the left in Figure 11.6. For time series data with defined date variables, you can select a range of dates and/or times based on the defined date variables, as shown on the right in Figure 11.6. For other data files, you can select a range of observation (row) numbers. To generate date variables for time series data, use the Define Dates option on the Data menu.

Figure 11.6 Select Cases Range dialog boxes

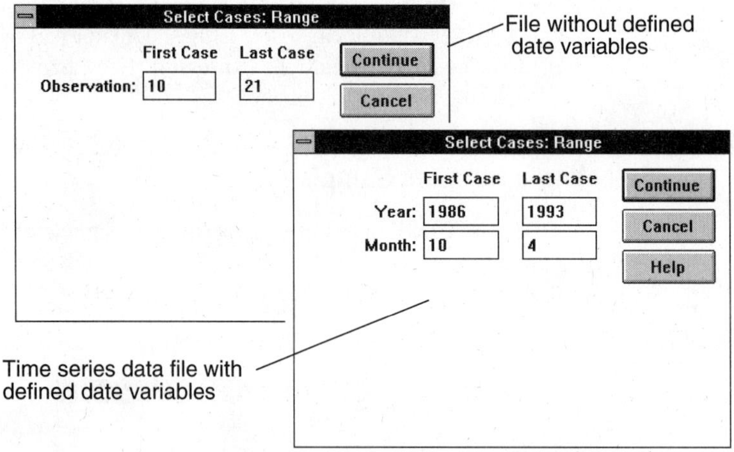

In a time series data file, each case represents observations at a different time, and the file is sorted in chronological order. To define date variables for time series data, use the Define Dates option on the Data menu.

First Case. Enter the starting date and/or time values for the range. If no date variables are defined, enter the starting observation number (row number in the Data Editor, unless Split File is on). If you don't specify a Last Case value, all cases from the starting date/time to the end of the time series are selected.

Last Case. Enter the ending date and/or time values for the range. If no date variables are defined, enter the ending observation number (row number in the Data Editor, unless Split File is on). If you don't specify a First Case value, all cases from the beginning of the time series up to the ending date/time are selected.

Case Selection Status

If you have selected a subset of cases but have not discarded unselected cases, unselected cases are marked in the Data Editor with a diagonal line through the row number, as shown in Figure 11.7.

Figure 11.7 Case selection status

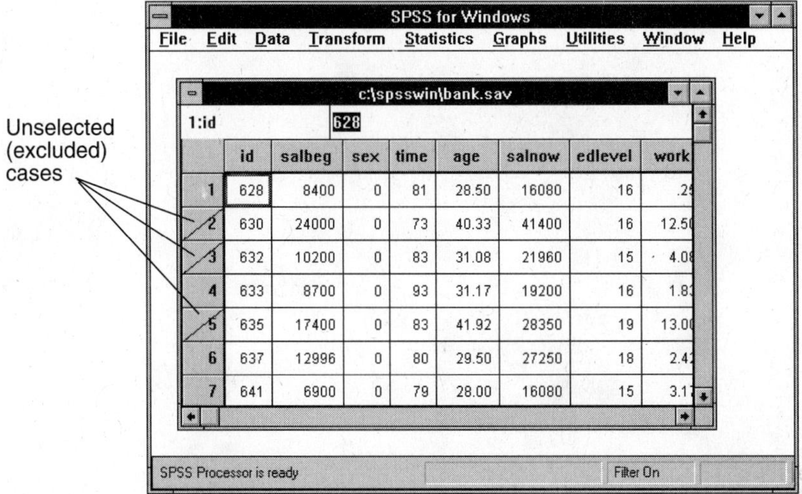

12 Additional Statistical Procedures

This chapter contains brief tutorials for selected statistical procedures. It also suggests some examples for exploring other procedures. The procedures are grouped according to the order in which they appear on the Statistics menu.

The examples are designed to illustrate sample specifications required to run a statistical procedure. Most of the examples use the *employee.sav* file, which is described in Chapter 4. The exponential smoothing example uses the *inventor.sav* file, which contains inventory data collected over a period of 70 days. In the examples in this chapter, you must run the procedures to see the output.

For further information about individual items in a dialog box, click on Help. If you want to locate a specific statistic (for example, percentiles), use the Search facility in the Help system, as described in Chapter 2. For further information on how to interpret the results obtained by running these procedures, consult a statistics or data analysis textbook.

Summarizing Data

The Summarize submenu on the Statistics menu provides techniques for summarizing data with statistics and charts. Following are brief tutorials for the Frequencies and Explore procedures.

Frequencies

An example showing a frequency table and a bar chart is provided in Chapter 1. In that example, the Frequencies procedure was used to analyze the variable *jobcat*, which has a small number of distinct job categories. If the variable you want to analyze has a large number of different values, you can use the Frequencies procedure to generate summary statistics and a histogram. A **histogram** is a chart that shows the number of cases in each of several groups. To generate statistics and a histogram of the current salaries in the *employee.sav* file, follow these steps:

❶ From the menus choose:

Statistics
 Summarize ▸
  Frequencies...

This opens the Frequencies dialog box, as shown on the left in Figure 12.1.

Figure 12.1 Frequencies dialog boxes

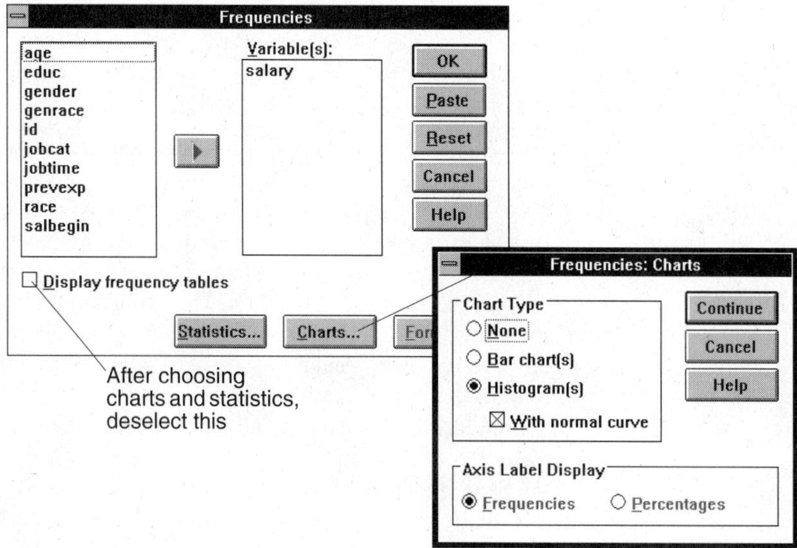

❷ Select *salary* as a variable.

❸ Click on Charts... to open the Frequencies Charts dialog box, as shown on the right in Figure 12.1.

❹ Select Histogram(s) and With normal curve, and then click on Continue.

❺ To select summary statistics, click on Statistics... in the Frequencies dialog box. Select Mean, Std. deviation, and Maximum in the Frequencies Statistics dialog box, and then click on Continue.

❻ Deselect Display frequency tables in the main Frequencies dialog box.

(If you leave this item selected and display a frequency table for current salary, the output shows an entry for every distinct value of salary, making a very long table.)

❼ Click on OK to run the procedure.

The output window shows the requested statistics. The histogram is displayed in the Chart Carousel. Each bar in the histogram represents the number of employees within a salary range, and the salary values displayed are the range midpoints. As requested, a normal curve is superimposed on the chart.

Explore

Suppose you want to look further at the distribution of salary for each job category in the *employee.sav* file. With the Explore procedure, you can examine the distribution of salary within categories of another variable.

❶ From the menus choose:

Statistics
  Summarize ▸
    Explore...

This opens the Explore dialog box, as shown in Figure 12.2.

Figure 12.2 Explore dialog box

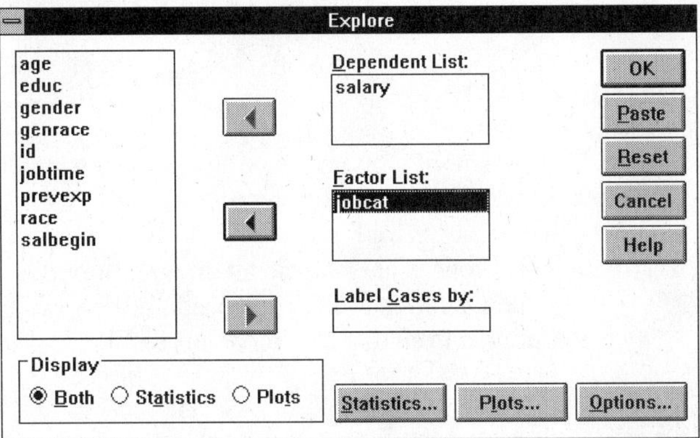

❷ Select *salary* for the Dependent List.

❸ Select *jobcat* for the Factor List.

❹ Click on OK to run the Explore procedure.

In the output, descriptive statistics and a stem-and-leaf plot are displayed for the current salaries in each job category. The Chart Carousel contains a boxplot comparing the salaries in the job categories. For each category, the boxplot shows the median, interquartile range (25th to 75th percentile), outliers (indicated by O), and extreme values (indicated by *).

More about Summarizing Data

SPSS has many choices for summarizing data. To calculate medians or percentiles, use the Frequencies procedure or the Explore procedure. The following list suggests some ways in which you can experiment with additional procedures to summarize data.

- **Descriptives.** For current salary, you can calculate standard scores, sometimes called **Z scores**. Use the Descriptives procedure and select Save standardized values as variables.
- **Crosstabs.** Instead of making one table, as in the example of the Crosstabs procedure in Chapter 4, you can create separate tables for males and females by moving *gender* into the layer box and selecting *race* as the column variable.
- **List Cases.** You can use the List Cases procedure to write to your output window a listing of the actual values of gender, job category, and current salary of the first 25 or 50 employees.

Comparing Means

The Compare Means submenu on the Statistics menu provides techniques for displaying descriptive statistics and testing whether differences are significant between two means for both independent and paired samples. You can also test whether differences are significant among more than two independent means by using the One-Way ANOVA procedure. Following are brief tutorials using two procedures from this group, Means and Paired-Samples T Test.

Means

In the employee data file, several variables are available for dividing the employees into groups. You can calculate various statistics to compare the groups. For example, you can compute the average (mean) salaries for white and minority males and females. To calculate the means, use the following steps:

1. From the menus choose:

   Statistics
   Compare Means ▸
   Means...

This opens the Means dialog box, as shown in Figure 12.3.

Figure 12.3 Means dialog box (layer 1)

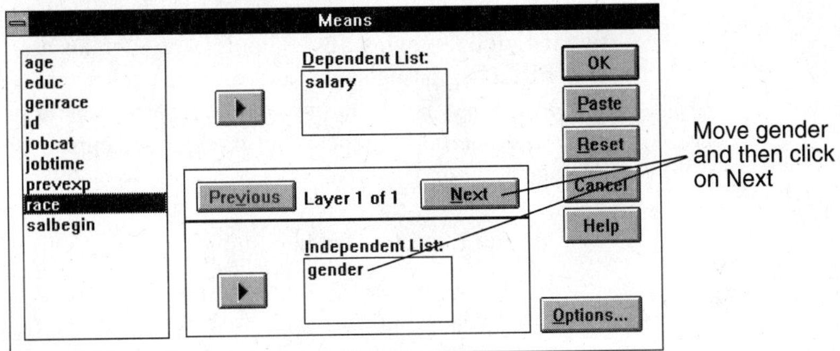

❷ Select *salary* for the Dependent Lis t.

❸ Select *gender* for the Independent List in layer 1.

❹ Click on Next. This creates another layer, as shown in Figure 12.4.

Figure 12.4 Means dialog box (layer 2)

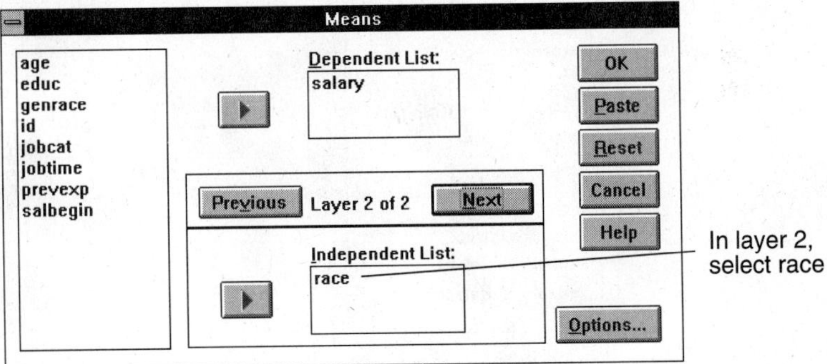

❺ Select *race* for the Independent List in layer 2.

❻ Click on OK to run the procedure.

The output displays the mean salary for the entire group of employees, the mean salaries for males and females (layer 1), and the mean salaries for white males, minority males, white females, and minority females (layer 2). The standard deviations and the number of cases in each category are also displayed in the table.

Paired-Samples T Test

When the data are structured in such a way that there are two observations on the same individual or observations that are matched by another variable on two individuals (twins, for example), the samples are paired. In the employee data file, a beginning salary and a current salary are listed for each employee. If the company is prospering, periodic raises would probably be granted, and you would certainly expect that the average current salary is greater than the average beginning salary.

To carry out a *t* test of the beginning salary and current salary means, use the following steps:

1. From the menus choose:

   Statistics
     Compare Means ▶
       Paired-Samples T Test...

   This opens the Paired-Samples T Test dialog box, as shown in Figure 12.5.

Figure 12.5 Paired-Samples T Test dialog box

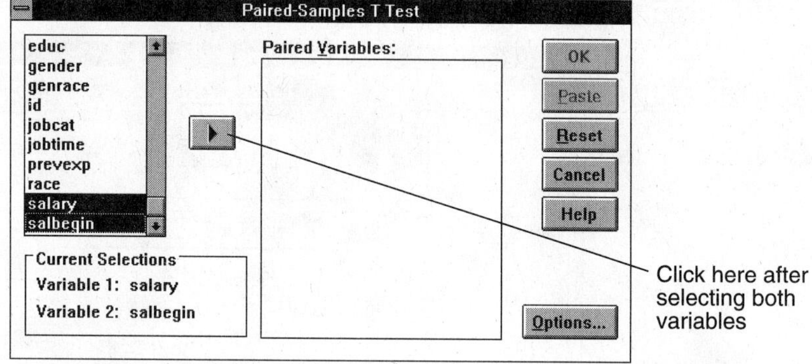

2. Click on *salary*. The variable is displayed in the Current Selections group.
3. Click on *salbegin*. The variable is displayed in the Current Selections group.
4. Click on ▶ to move the pair to the Paired Variables list.
5. Click on OK to run the procedure.

The results, as expected, show that the current salary is significantly different from the beginning salary, as indicated by the small probability displayed in the *2-tail Sig* column. The data structure in this example is similar to an experiment in which the same person is observed before and after an intervention.

More about Comparing Means

The following examples suggest some ways in which you can use other procedures to compare means.

- **Independent-Samples T Test.** When you use a *t* test to compare means of one variable across independent groups, the samples are independent. Males and females in the employee file can be divided into independent groups by the variable *gender.* You can use a *t* test to determine if the mean current salaries of males and females are the same.
- **One-Sample T Test.** You can test whether the average salary of clerical workers in this company differs from a national or state average. Use Select Cases... on the Data menu to select the cases with *jobcat*=1. Then, run the One-Sample T Test procedure to compare *salary* and the test value 35000.
- **One-Way ANOVA.** The variable *genrace* divides employees into four independent groups by gender and race. You can use the One-Way ANOVA procedure to test whether mean beginning salaries for the four groups are significantly different.

ANOVA Models

The ANOVA Models submenu on the Statistics menu provides techniques for testing univariate analysis-of-variance models. (If you have only one factor, you can use the One-Way ANOVA procedure on the Compare Means submenu.)

Simple Factorial ANOVA

The Simple Factorial ANOVA procedure performs an analysis of variance for factorial designs. A simple factorial design can be used to test if employees with differing race and gender classifications have the same beginning salaries.

❶ From the menus choose:

Statistics
  ANOVA Models ▸
    Simple Factorial...

This opens the Simple Factorial ANOVA dialog box, as shown on the left in Figure 12.6.

Figure 12.6 Simple Factorial ANOVA dialog box

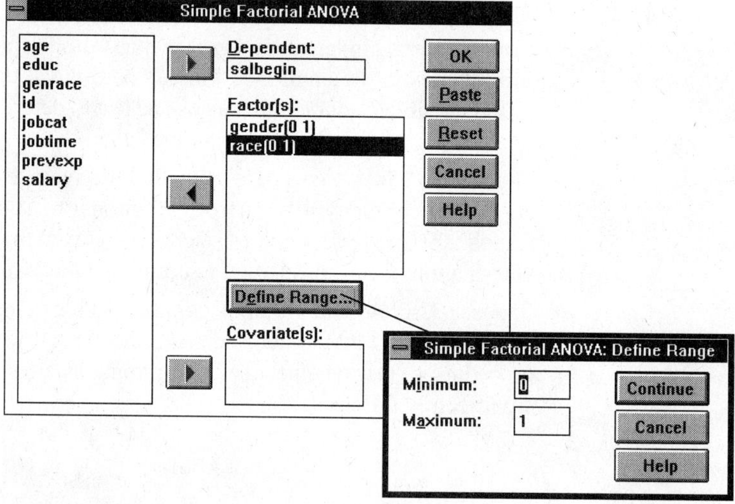

2 Select *salbegin* as the dependent variable.

3 Select *gender* and *race* as factors.

4 With *gender* and *race* selected, click on Define Range....

This opens the Define Range dialog box, as shown on the right in Figure 12.6.

5 Type **0** in the Minimum text box and **1** in the Maximum text box. Then click on Continue.

For *gender*, the value 0 is the code for male and the value 1 is the code for female. For *race*, the value 0 is the code for white and the value 1 is the code for minority.

In any dialog box, you can click the right mouse button on any variable to pop up information about that variable.

Hint: If you don't know the range for a variable, click on it with the *right* mouse button to pop up a variable information window. (To do this, you will temporarily need to cancel the Define Range dialog box.)

6 Click on OK to run the procedure.

In the output, you can see that the effects of *gender* and *race* are definitely significant and that the observed significance level of the interaction of *gender* and *race* is 0.014. For further interpretation, consult a statistics or data analysis textbook.

Recoding variables. The factor variable must be a numeric variable with a small number of discrete values. To recode a string variable, select Automatic

Recode... from the Transform menu. For example, you can recode a string variable designating type of municipal bond funds (general, high yield, etc.) into a new variable containing code numbers for the types.

To recode a continuous numeric variable into a small number of groups, select Recode from the Transform menu. Chapter 7 shows how to recode the variable *salary* into a new variable containing only three discrete salary ranges.

Correlating Variables

The Correlate submenu on the Statistics menu provides measures of association for two or more numeric variables. Following are an example of the Bivariate Correlation procedure and a brief tutorial using the Partial Correlations procedure.

Bivariate Correlations

You can calculate a Pearson correlation coefficient to see if there is a linear association between *salary* (current salary) and *salbegin* (beginning salary).

Partial Correlations

The Partial Correlations procedure calculates partial correlation coefficients that describe the relationship between two variables while adjusting for the effects of one or more additional variables.

You can estimate the correlation between *salbegin* and *salary*, controlling for the linear effects of *jobtime* (time on the job) and *prevexp* (previous experience). The number of control variables determines the order of the partial correlation coefficient.

❶ From the menus choose:

Statistics
 Correlate ▸
  Partial...

This opens the Partial Correlations dialog box, as shown in Figure 12.7.

Figure 12.7 Partial Correlations dialog box

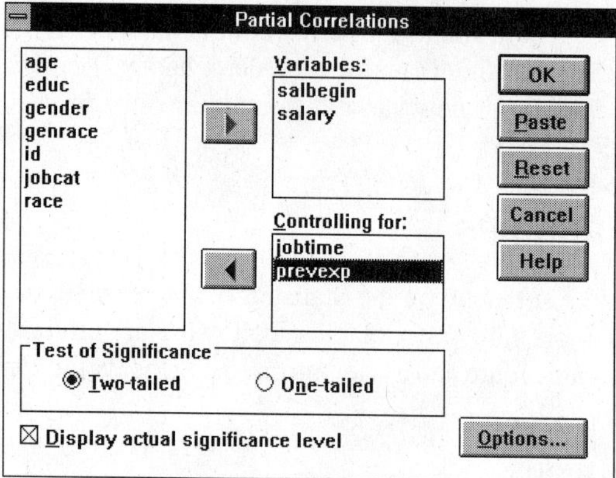

2. Select *salbegin* and *salary* as variables.
3. Select *jobtime* and *prevexp* as control variables.
4. Click on OK to run the procedure.

The output shows a table of partial correlation coefficients, the number of cases, and the significance level for the pair *salary* and *salbegin*.

Regression Analysis

The Regression submenu on the Statistics menu provides regression techniques, including curve estimation. Following is a brief tutorial using the Linear Regression procedure.

Linear Regression

The Linear Regression procedure examines the relationship between a dependent variable and a set of independent variables. You can use it to predict an employee's current salary (the dependent variable) from independent variables such as number of years of education, months of experience, gender, and race.

1. From the menus choose:

Statistics
  Regression ▸
    Linear...

This opens the Linear Regression dialog box, as shown in Figure 12.8.

Figure 12.8 Linear Regression dialog box

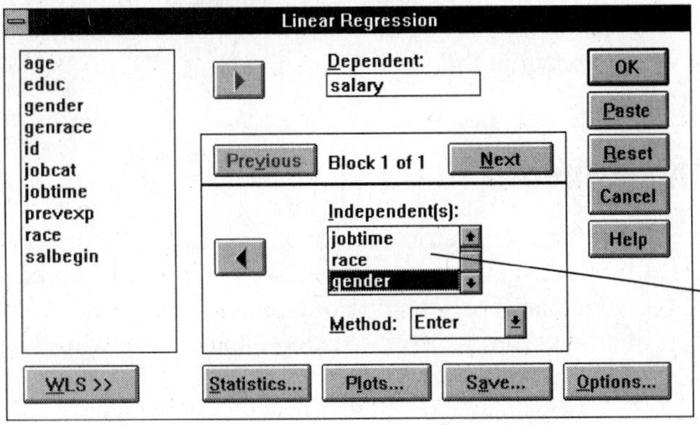

Select educ, jobtime, race, and gender as independent variables

2. Select *salary* as the dependent variable.
3. Select *educ*, *jobtime*, *race*, and *gender* as the independent variables.
4. Click on OK to run the procedure.

The output contains goodness-of-fit statistics and the coefficients for the variables. By examining the significance column, you can see that *jobtime* should not be in the equation.

Examining fit. To see how well the regression model fits your data, you can examine the residuals and other types of diagnostics that this procedure provides. In the Linear Regression dialog box, click on Save... to see a list of the new variables you can add to your data file. If you generate any of these variables, they will not be available in a later SPSS session unless you save the data file.

Methods. If you have collected a large number of independent variables and want to build a regression model that includes only variables that are statistically related to the dependent variable, you can select a method from the drop-down list. For example, if you select Stepwise in the above example, only variables that meet the criteria in the Linear Regression Options dialog box are entered in the equation, and the output lists *jobtime* under Variables not in the Equation.

More about Regression Procedures

The following example uses another regression procedure:

- **Curve Estimation.** You can use the Curve Estimation procedure to fit linear, quadratic, and cubic models of *salary* as a function of *salbegin*.

To use the Curve Estimation procedure for predictions for time series data, in the Independent group, select Time and then click on Save.... Select Predicted values and Predict through. Make entries in the Curve Estimation Save dialog box similar to the entries described for prediction in "Exponential Smoothing" on p. 103.

Nonparametric Tests

The Nonparametric Tests submenu on the Statistics menu provides nonparametric tests for one sample or for two or more paired or independent samples. Nonparametric tests do not require assumptions about the shape of the distributions from which the data originate. Following is a brief tutorial using the Chi-Square Test procedure.

Chi-Square

The Chi-Square Test procedure is used to test hypotheses about the relative proportion of cases falling into several mutually exclusive groups. You can test the hypothesis that employees in the company occur in the same proportions of gender and race as the general population in a certain county (white males 40%, minority males 10%, white females 40%, and minority females 10%).

❶ From the menus choose:

Statistics
  Nonparametric Tests ▸
    Chi-Square...

This opens the Chi-Square Test dialog box, as shown in Figure 12.9.

Figure 12.9 Chi-Square Test dialog box

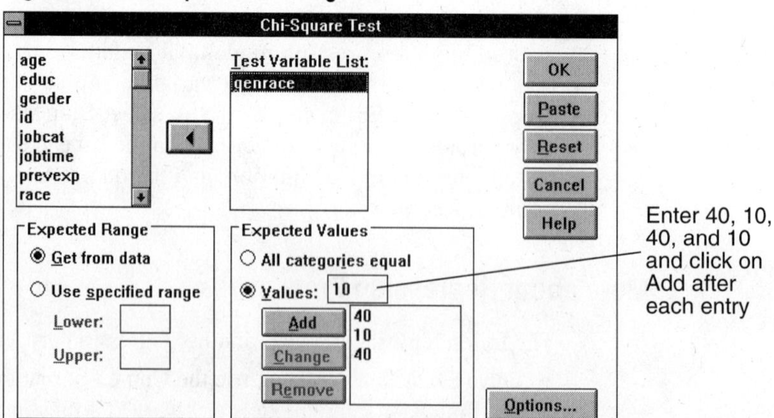

❷ Select *genrace* as the test variable.

❸ Click on Values in the Expected Values group.

❹ Type **40** in the Values text box and click on Add.

❺ Type **10** in the Values text box and click on Add.

❻ Repeat step ❹ and step ❺.

❼ Click on OK to run the procedure.

The output shows a table of the expected and residual values for the categories. The chi-square test shows a significant difference.

Time Series Analysis

A **time series variable** is a variable whose values are recorded at regular intervals over a period of time. The Time Series submenu on the Statistics menu provides exponential smoothing that can be used for predictions. Following is a brief tutorial using the Exponential Smoothing procedure.

Exponential Smoothing

The Exponential Smoothing procedure performs exponential smoothing of time series data. It creates new series containing predicted values and residuals.

For example, you can fit a model for inventory data and use it to predict the next week's inventory. Suppose that for 70 days you have kept track of the inventory of power supplies and that you want to construct a model and then use it to forecast power supplies for the next week.

❶ Open the *inventor.sav* file. (It is in the directory where SPSS is installed.)

❷ From the menus choose:

Statistics
 Time Series ▸
  Exponential Smoothing...

This opens the Exponential Smoothing dialog box, as shown in Figure 12.10.

Figure 12.10 Exponential Smoothing dialog box

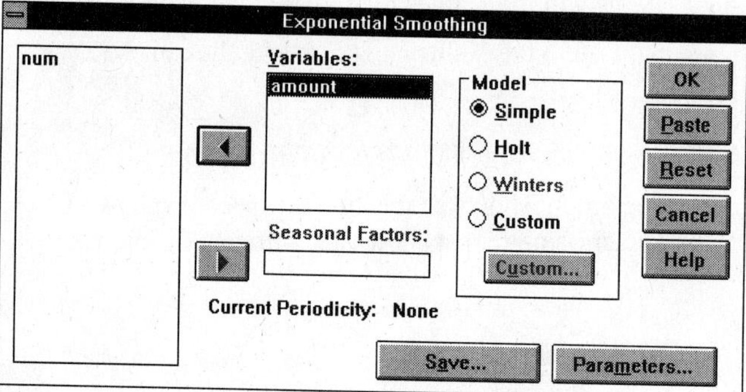

❸ Select *amount* for the Variables list.

❹ Click on Parameters... to specify the procedure.

This opens the Exponential Smoothing Parameters dialog box, as shown in Figure 12.11.

Figure 12.11 Exponential Smoothing Parameters dialog box

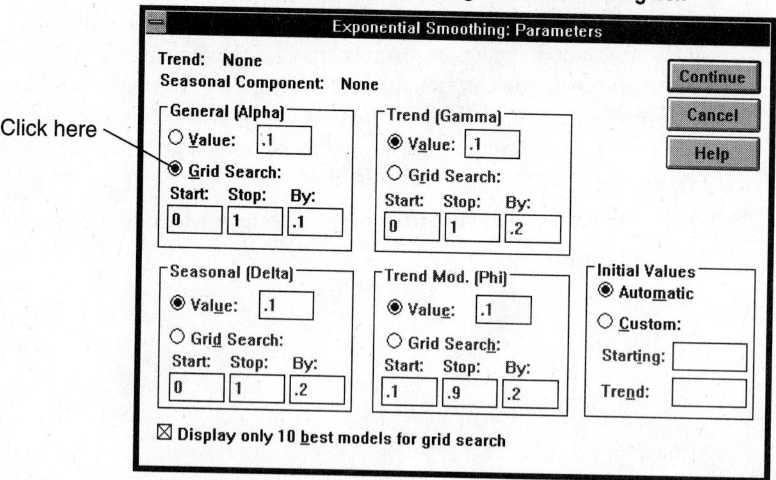

❺ To search for the best general parameter, click on Grid Search and then click on Continue.

❻ To create a new variable that contains predicted values, click on Save....

This opens the Exponential Smoothing Save dialog box, as shown in Figure 12.12.

Figure 12.12 Exponential Smoothing Save dialog box

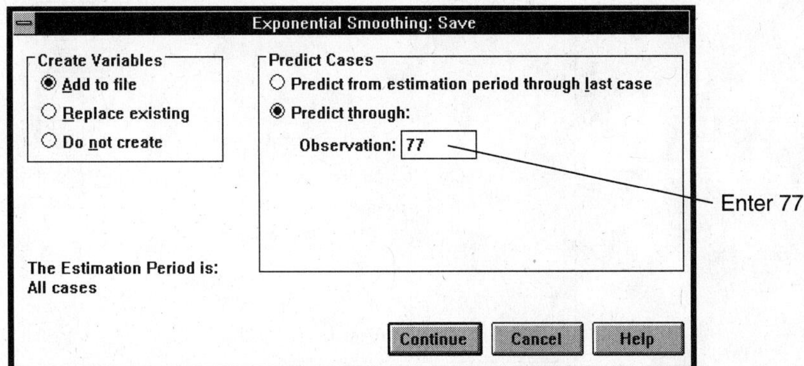

❼ Click on Predict through and type **77** in the Observation text box.

This adds 7 days to the original 70.

❽ Click on Continue and then in the main dialog box, click on OK.

This runs the procedure and adds new variables *fit_1* and *err_1*. The variable *fit_1* contains the fitted values and the seven new predicted values. The variable *err_1* contains residual values for the original 70 cases; you can use the residuals for further analysis. If you want to save the new variables, select Save As... from the File menu and save the data file under a new name.

❾ To see a chart of the original data and the new fit line, from the menus choose:

Graphs
  Sequence...

This opens the Sequence Charts dialog box, as shown in Figure 12.13.

Figure 12.13 Sequence Charts dialog box

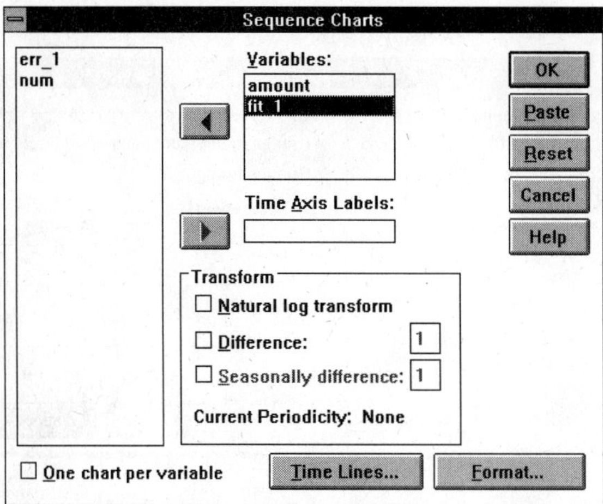

⑩ Select *amount* and *fit_1* as variables.

⑪ Click on OK to run the procedure.

The resulting chart shows both the actual number of power supplies and the fit line plotted on the same axes. The predicted values are plotted for the next week at the right side of the chart.

Index